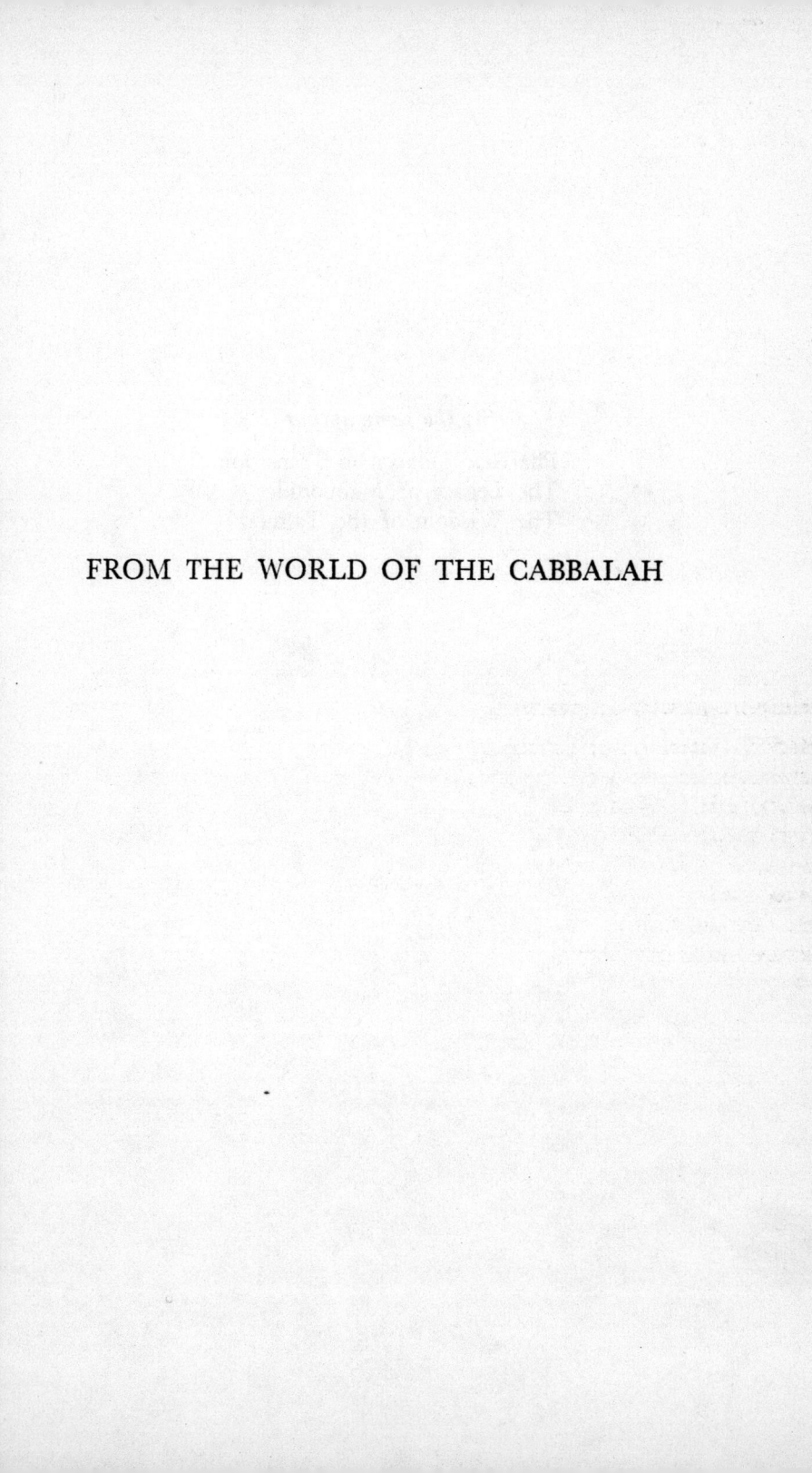

FROM THE WORLD OF THE CABBALAH

By the same author

Pharisaic Judaism in Transition
The Legacy of Maimonides
The Wisdom of the Talmud

FROM THE WORLD OF THE CABBALAH

The Philosophy of Rabbi Judah Loew of Prague

By
RABBI BEN ZION BOKSER

PHILOSOPHICAL LIBRARY
New York

COPYRIGHT, 1954, BY
THE PHILOSOPHICAL LIBRARY, INC.
15 EAST 40TH STREET, NEW YORK, N. Y.

PRINTED IN THE UNITED STATES OF AMERICA

To the memory of my beloved teachers, Dr. Louis Ginzberg and Dr. Alexander Marx, who proved by their lives that the study of the Torah is indeed without measure.

Table of Contents

Preface		ix
I	The World of the Cabbalah	1
II	A Portrait of the Master	15
	1. The Origin of Rabbi Judah	17
	2. The Culture of the Sixteenth Century	22
	3. Jewish Life in Bohemia and Poland	28
	4. Conflict and Achievement	35
III	Human Destiny	51
	1. The Legends about the Golem	55
	2. The Divine Character of Life	59
	3. On the Nature of Man	69
	4. The Upward Path	73
	5. The Foundations of World Order	84
	6. On Vindicating Creation	90
IV	Reason and Faith	93
	1. The Challenge of Rationalism	97
	2. Reason Has Her Limits	103
	3. On Reaching for the Ultimate	108
	4. The Autonomy of Faith	115
	5. The Cabbalah and the Interpretation of Scripture	126
	6. Education and Life	133
V	Judaism and Christianity	147
	1. The Humanists and Judaism	151
	2. The Battle of Scriptural Texts	156
	3. The Messianic Hope and the Doctrine of Time	171
	4. In Defense of the Talmud	178
VI	The Legacy of Rabbi Judah	185
Notes		195
Index		205

PREFACE

Rabbi Judah Loew of Prague lived and worked during the sixteenth century, the classic epoch of humanism. A pious and learned rabbi, an exponent of the wisdom of the Cabbalah, he was at the same time responsive to all the currents of thought which were at play in his time. He did his work among his own people, for the most part in the ghetto of Prague, but there are no walls against a free spirit in action. Rabbi Judah's world, as his writings reveal him, was the larger European community, with all its intellectual ferment, then at work to shape the modern mind. And Rabbi Judah's thought remains strikingly cogent for coping with the problems which the modern temper has engendered in the world.

The material here offered formed the basis of a series of lectures delivered at the Institute for Religious and Social Studies of the Jewish Theological Seminary of America. The first two chapters are introductory and are based on standard studies of the subject. The later chapters, portraying the thought of Rabbi Loew, form the main portion of the present work. They are based on an examination of the original writings of Rabbi Loew.

The author is indebted to Dr. Louis Finkelstein, whose interest led him to undertake the present study, and to Dr. Leo Strauss, Dr. Jacob B. Agus, Dr. Gershom G. Scholem, and Dr. Salo Baron for many helpful criticisms. He is thankful to Mr. Joseph Mindel for suggesting a number of stylistic revisions, to Mildred Shapiro, to Sarah Kurzman, and to Gabriella Landau for assistance with the typing of the manuscript, and to Mr. Jesse Fuchs for help in proofreading.

I
The World of the Cabbalah

THE WORLD OF THE CABBALAH

"I THANK GOD everyday that I was not born before the Zohar was revealed, for it was the Zohar which sustained me in my faith as a Jew." This tribute to the great classic of the Cabbalah was paid by one of the celebrated masters of *hasidism*, Rabbi Pinhas of Koretz[1] (died about 1791). It is an indication of the profound influence which Cabbalistic mysticism has had in the history of Judaism.

The term Cabbalah derives from the Hebrew, and its literal meaning is a *receiving* or a tradition. It stands, however, for a special branch of Jewish tradition. It is a body of teachings concerning God and the universe, in which God's contact with His creation is conceived in terms of immediacy and nearness. These teachings were usually surrounded by secrecy, and they were transmitted orally or in a highly veiled literature, which proceeds by hints rather than by explicit declarations.

The secrecy surrounding the Cabbalah was born of the awareness that its ideas were much too subtle for the average mind. Its daring interpretations of religion and life, expressed in an unfamiliar symbolism often lent itself to misunderstanding. When the fundamental concepts of religion were at stake, one could not proceed except with caution. The Cabbalists believed, moreover, that their doctrines endowed man with mystical powers by which he might control nature herself. Such powers could not be entrusted to random individuals. Those who sought to study the Cabbalah had to be screened, therefore, to make certain that they would not invoke their powers too casually or for ignoble ends. Thus there developed the conviction that only certain chosen spirits in each generation were worthy of being the recipients of the wisdom of the Cabbalah.

What are the central ideas in the wisdom of the Cabbalah?

[1]

FROM THE WORLD OF THE CABBALAH

The Cabbalah does not present itself to the world as a totally new doctrine. It offers itself instead as an interpretation of traditional concepts in religion. What was the significance of the Biblical stories, of the laws and customs ordained in Scripture? In the stage of innocence, before man's religious world had been invaded by the spirit of sophistication, this question was never really raised. Every prescription in the Torah was sacred, and it was sacred by reference to its own literal meaning. Whatever is in the Torah is God's will, and as such must always command our highest loyalty.

Conventional Jewish piety was of this order. It fulfilled itself in the observance of the traditional rituals, and in the study of the Torah, especially the vast literature of the Talmud. Man's simple acceptance of traditional religion was, however, shattered by sophistication, by philosophy. It was shattered by the teachings of the Greeks, principally Aristotle, who taught a naturalistic view of the universe, in which reason and its fruit, the various sciences, offer us the only clue to truth.

A school of mediators arose, the greatest of whom was Moses Maimonides, who tried to justify the teachings of the Torah by the canons of reason. Maimonides interpreted the Biblical text figuratively, and he justified the laws of the Torah on the grounds of their utility. As Maimonides put it: "Every one of the six hundred and thirteen precepts serve to inculcate some truth, to remove some erroneous opinion, to establish proper relations in society, to diminish evil, to train us in good manners, or to warn us against bad habits."[2] He conceded to the Greeks that the knowledge of science and the conclusions established by the metaphysician are an indispensable step to the truth we need to know about God. God is thus to be known indirectly, only through a knowledge of the vast order of creation, as it is unfolded to us by the act of reason.

The work of these mediators represented a formidable achievement, but there were many who were left cold by it. Indeed, there were some who felt that the marriage of convenience between Greek thought and the teachings of the Torah had brought together irreconcilable elements. This "synthesis" had reduced religion to a philosophy. It had made the knowledge of God dependent on the laborious work of reason. It had reduced the commandments of the Torah to utilitarian prescriptions. How could this satisfy the human heart which sought to feel the exaltation of closeness to a God who loved man and wanted to guide him toward a beneficent destiny?

The impatience with rationalism has always been a characteristic of more romantic temperaments, who want to adore rather than to analyze, who insist that we can know the whole by our sympathies and feelings, without necessarily breaking up that whole into its fragments, for the minute analysis of each part. This is the way of mysticism. The Cabbalah was an exploration of the mystical way. Its cause was the quest for God as an object of direct experience, without the mediating services of metaphysics.

The Cabbalists were interested in the natural world, and they speculated on the significance of the Biblical narratives and laws. But they were not interested in reconciling their knowledge of nature with the theories of Aristotle. They developed the conviction that nature is but an outer garb of an immaterial divine essence. They looked upon the visible facts of existence as but the final stage in a process of materialization whose highest source is the ineffable, incomprehensible divine Being in whom there is no materiality, and none of the attributes of materiality. God, they taught, reaches down to us through a graded chain of being, proceeding from His own ineffable self, and moving through spheres of immaterial divine forces called *sefirot* which emanate from Him. In their final unfolding the *sefirot* beget the visible elements of the material universe.

The same theory was applied to the texts of the Torah. Maimonides had drawn striking parallels between the legal system of the Torah and the laws governing the order of nature.[3] The Torah was a divinely inspired document, a creation of God, in other words, as was everything else in existence. The Cabbalists operated with the same parallelism. The Biblical narratives and laws, the literal text, these were the material expressions of the divine idea, achieved through an intermediary, the *sefirot*. In the Torah as in every other of God's works the same creative process had been at work. The immaterial had robed itself in the material. God's ineffable self had reached down to man in an act of materialization and concretion. From God, through the *sefirot*, to the realm of concrete existence—these are the crucial stages in the great epic of creation.

The Cabbalists believed that tokens of God's presence are discernible throughout creation, in the physical facts of nature, as well as in the physical word of the Torah. Much of the labor of the Cabbalists was a search for these tokens. It was an effort to penetrate the outer garment to see the inner essence. It was a search for the "signs" of the divine dimension of life which lay scattered in the physical facts of existence, in nature as in the Torah.

The most striking doctrine of the Cabbalah was that of the *sefirot*. This was an attempt to overcome the paradox between the conception of God as infinite Being Who is therefore beyond involvement in the flux of existence, beyond desire and change, and the God Who participates in the drama of life, the God Who is the central figure in the processes of creation, revelation and redemption. The Cabbalists met this problem by assuming two levels of being in God. In his own innermost and essential Being, God is incomprehensible, beyond all characterization, and beyond all contact with the created universe. He is the *En Sof*, the Infinite, the Boundless One. But then God manifests Himself in ten successive spheres of activity. These ten *sefirot*, as Gershom G. Scholem put it, represent "spheres of divine manifestation in which God emerges from His hidden abode. . . . All mundane and created things exist only because something of the power of the *sefirot* lives and acts in them." [4]

FROM THE WORLD OF THE CABBALAH

The Cabbalists used all kinds of imagery to convey their meaning. As the Zohar phrased it: "The Aged of all the aged, the Unknown of all the unknown has form and yet has no form. He has a form whereby the universe is preserved, and yet has no form, because He cannot be comprehended. When he first assumed the form (of the first *sefirah*) He caused nine splendid lights to emanate from it which, shining through it, diffused a bright light in all directions. Imagine an elevated light sending forth its rays in all directions. If we approach it to examine the rays, we understand no more than that they emanate from the said light. So is the Holy Aged an absolute light, but in Himself concealed and incomprehensible. We can only comprehend Him through those luminous emanations (*sefirot*) which are partly visible and partly concealed. These constitute the sacred name of God." [5]

The process by which the *sefirot* arose and by which they did their work in creation remained an intriguing problem for the Cabbalists. The common human experience of procreation suggested the union of a male and female principle. The Cabbalists accordingly identified the *sefirot* as male and female, and they explained their fructifying power in life as the fruit of their union. All these conceptions they usually read into the Biblical text through an ingenious method of interpretation.

Cabbalistic literature often attempts to define the ten *sefirot*. The first *sefirah* usually called *Keter*, "crown," is the highest realm of divinity in action. It is identical with the primeval will of God. The first *sefirah* contained within itself, as a potentiality, the entire universe. From *Keter*, which is an absolute unity, differentiated from everything that is manifold or compounded, proceed two parallel principles, which seem opposed but are in fact complementary, the one masculine, active, called *Hokmah*, or "wisdom," and the other feminine, passive called *Binah*, or "intellect." The juncture of these two, sometimes designated as "father" and "mother," engendered the remaining seven *sefirot*. As the Zohar expresses it: "When the Holy Aged, the Concealed of all concealed, assumed a form, He produced everything as either male or female. Hence 'wisdom' (*Hokmah,* which initiates the chain of development), when it derived from the Holy Aged, emanated in a male and female expression, for 'wisdom' expanded and 'intellect' proceeded from it; and thus obtained male and female: 'wisdom,' the father, and 'intellect' the mother, from whose union the other pairs of *sefirot* emanated."

The seven remaining *sefirot* which follow are designated as *Hesed* or "mercy," *Din* or "judgment," *Tiferet* or "beauty," *Nezah* or "triumph," *Hod* or "glory," *Yesod* or "foundation," and *Malkut* or "kingdom." The Cabbalah abounds in efforts to define the realities corresponding to these *sefirot.* The last *sefirah, Malkut,* designates the stage of materialization, when the concrete universe is finally brought into being.

The elaborate imagery employed by the Cabbalists was necessitated by the subtlety of their ideas. But even their imagery did not altogether remove the paradox of the Infinite translating Himself into the finite. It was undoubtedly the awareness of this difficulty which helped make the Cabbalists so reticent about teaching their doctrines to the general public.

We shall now proceed with the literary history of the Cabbalah. The Cabbalists had as their forerunners the teachers of the Talmud and Midrash who endeavored to probe into the mysteries of God's being. They usually based their speculations on the Biblical story of creation, and on the prophet Ezekiel's account of his vision of God. Their speculations were pursued as a secret doctrine, and they divulged their thoughts only to certain duly qualified people, in private sessions with one or two at a time. As the Mishnah, in a cryptic passage testifies: "The work of creation may not be expounded in the presence of two, nor the work of the chariot (Ezekiel's vision of God as reported in ch.1:4f, ch.10, and Isaiah's vision of God in ch.6) in the presence of one, unless he is a sage and can follow with his own understanding. Whoever speculates on four things, it would have been better if he had not come into

FROM THE WORLD OF THE CABBALAH

the world; what is above, what is beneath, what before, and what after." [6]

The earliest systematic development of the Cabbalah is presented in the *Sefer Yezirah* or the *Book of Creation*. It was written between the third and sixth centuries. It traces God's creative presence to the harmonies of numbers and their equivalent symbols in the Hebrew alphabet. Joining the primary numbers from one to ten and the twenty-two letters of the Hebrew alphabet, we get "thirty-two secret paths of wisdom," as this book describes it, through which God created all that has existence. The ten primary numbers are here called *sefirot*, and it is from this text that the concept of the *sefirot* was introduced to the later Cabbalah. Another text which was also produced in antiquity, was the *Shiur Komah* (*The Measure of the Heights*), a work on the dimensions of the Deity, which as the title suggests characterizes God in terms of gross corporeality.

In the ninth and tenth centuries, the center of the Cabbalah shifted from the East to Italy, Spain, Provence, and Germany. The early masters of Cabbalah in Europe include Isaac the Blind, who was active in the beginning of the 13th century, and his two disciples, Azariel and Ezra.

Isaac's writings are no longer extant, except as fragments quoted in other works. From these it is evident that he believed in the transmigration of souls. By looking into a man's face he felt himself able to determine whether an individual possessed an original soul, fresh from the spirit world, or whether his was a soul which had been in some other body and was now working its way toward perfection before being permitted to unite itself again with the realm of pure spirits.

Azariel was born in Valladolid about 1160, and he died in 1238. His work, *The Commentary on the Ten Sefirot*, presents its expositions by means of questions and answers and it embodies the earliest statement of the principal doctrines of the Cabbalah.

A disciple of Azariel and Ezra, who helped immensely in

FROM THE WORLD OF THE CABBALAH

the spread of Cabbalistic teachings was Moses ben Nahman (1194-1270). A practicing physician and an accomplished student of philosophy, Moses was also a widely recognized authority of the Talmud. But the Cabbalah had captured his soul and all his writings are tinged with Cabbalistic ideas.

Moses was born in Gerona, Spain, where he served both as rabbi and physician. Later on, he became chief rabbi of the province of Catalonia. In 1263, he was challenged to defend Judaism in a public disputation with Pablo Christiani, an apostate Jew who was now a representative of the Dominican order. The subjects on which they argued were: whether the Messiah had appeared; whether the Messiah announced by the prophets was to be considered as divine or as a man born of human parents; and whether the Jews or the Christians were in possession of the true faith. Freedom of utterance was granted to the disputants, and Moses expounded his views without hindrance. But when he later published the substance of his remarks in pamphlet form, he brought upon himself the ire of the authorities, and he was forced to flee for his life. In 1267 he emigrated to Palestine where he remained for the rest of his life.

The most important of the writings of Moses, from the point of view of the development of the Cabbalah, was his commentary on the Pentateuch, in which the Biblical text becomes a kind of allegory for all the subtle ideas of Cabbalistic mysticism.

A younger contemporary of Nahmanides who introduced an ascetic as well as ecstatic influence into the Cabbalah was Abraham ben Samuel Abulafia (1240-1292). Abulafia came to the Cabbalah only after he had become disillusioned with the more conventional interpretation of Judaism. He had mastered the study of Bible, Talmud, philosophy and medicine. The rationalism of Saadia and Maimonides did not satisfy him, and he finally became an adherent of the Cabbalah. But he was not content with explaining the world in terms of the *sefirot*. He sought to penetrate the spirit realm, to unite himself with

God, and thereby to attain the powers of prophecy. To qualify for this union with God, Abulafia adopted an ascetic regimen of living. Withdrawn from the world, dressed in white, immersed in prayer and meditation, uttering the divine name with special modulations of the voice and with special gestures, he induced in himself a state of ecstasy in which he believed the soul had shed its material bonds and, unimpeded, returned to its divine source. In such moments of ecstasy he felt himself possessed of the revelations of prophecy.

Abulafia believed that his system represented the highest expression of the Cabbalistic tradition, as may be gathered from his own words. "The Cabbalistic tradition," he wrote, "is divisible into two parts. . . . The first part is occupied with the knowledge of the Deity, obtained by means of the doctrine of the *sefirot,* as propounded in the *Sefer Yezirah.* The followers of this part are related to those philosophers who strive to know God from His works, and the Deity stands before them objectively as a light beaming into their understanding. . . . The second and more important part strives to know God by means of the twenty-two letters of the alphabet, from which together with the vowel points and accents, those sundry divine names are combined, which elevate the Cabbalists to the degree of prophecy, drawing out their spirit, and causing it to be united with God and to become one with the Deity."[7]

Abulafia believed that he had really attained the status of prophecy. In 1281, he reported a call from God to convert the Pope, Martin IV, to Judaism. He tried to follow that call, and was imprisoned for his labors. In 1284, he announced another revelation, according to which he himself was the Messiah who would restore Israel to the Holy Land in 1296. Thousands believed him, and they prepared themselves for the return to Palestine.

Abulafia was a prolific writer. He produced twenty-two prophetic treatises as well as numerous other works. Through these works as well as through his life, Abulafia exerted a profound influence on the history of the Cabbalah.

Another influential master of the early Cabbalah was the author of the book *Bahir*. His identity has remained unknown, but his work was edited in Provence during the 12th Century.

The most important work of the Cabbalah is the *Zohar*, which was circulated in the last quarter of the 13th century by Moses de Leon. It was ascribed by him to the well-known Talmudist, Rabbi Simeon ben Johai, and it does contain many older elements, but de Leon's editorship has been clearly demonstrated. It was written in Aramaic, in the form of a running commentary on the Pentateuch, with various appendices attached to it. The *Zohar* became the central text in the entire Cabbalistic literature; and it has remained to this day the most influential expression of Jewish mysticism.

The next great epoch in the Cabbalah was represented by a group of mystics who lived in Palestine, in the city of Safed, in the sixteenth Century. The great pre-occupation of this school of Cabbalists was the mystery of Israel's suffering in exile and the hope for the Messianic redemption. The most important of these was Isaac ben Solomon Ashkenazi Luria (1533-1572). He was born in Jerusalem, but raised by an uncle in Cairo, Egypt. In 1570, he settled in Safed. His studies in Talmud and rabbinic lore did not satisfy him, and he gradually withdrew from the world to lead the life of an ascetic, in meditation and prayer. He reported revelations which came to him from the prophet Elijah and from the ancient masters whom his soul met in heaven during his sleep. He finally felt himself to be the Messiah ben Joseph, the forerunner of the final deliverer, and he became a worker of miracles. Luria did not write any books but his disciples transmitted his teachings to posterity.

The popularization of Luria's work was achieved largely through the efforts of Chaim Vital (1543-1620). His *Etz Hayim* is a thorough exposition of Luria's system in the Cabbalah, and he labored on it for thirty years. Another leading figure in the Safed School of Cabbalists was Moses Cardobero (1522-1570) whose work *Pardes Rimonim* (A Garden of Pomegranates) is likewise a major exposition of Cabbalistic ideas.

The Cabbalah became one of the spiritual sources of the popular mysticism known as *hasidism* which flourished in the 18th and 19th centuries, especially in Eastern Europe.[8]

The Cabbalah also found adherents in the Christian community. The father of the Christian Cabbalah was Pico della Mirandola. He pursued his studies under a Jew, Johanan Aleman. His nine hundred *Theses* which he published in 1486, at the age of twenty-four, included this bold declaration: "No science yields greater proof of the divinity of Christ than magic and Cabbalah." Pope Sixtus IV was so delighted with his work that he urged him to translate Cabbalistic texts into Latin for the use of divinity students. Mirandola translated the following three works: Menahem di Recanti's commentary on the Bible, Eliezer of Worms' *Hokmat ha-Nefesh* and Shem Tob Falaquera's *Sefer ha-Maalot*.

John Reuchlin studied Hebrew and Cabbalah under the Jewish court physician of Frederick III, Rabbi Jacob ben Jehiel Loanz. His first Cabbalistic treatise *De Verbo Mirifico* was published in Basel in 1494. Twenty-two years later he published his *De Arte Cabalistica*, which was a more mature exposition of the same basic ideas. These works made Reuchlin the most talked of man of letters in Europe, whose writings were read avidly in Protestant and Catholic circles alike.

Paracelsus did not write books on the Cabbalah as such. But he applied the insights of the Cabbalah to his own scientific and philosophic studies. His attitude toward the Cabbalah is stated clearly, and it is typical of what the leading intellectual lights of Europe believed: "The art of the Cabbalah is beholden to God, it is in alliance with Him, and it is founded in the words of Christ."[9]

The Christian Cabbalah differed from the Jewish model which inspired it, but both are essentially similar in conception.

FROM THE WORLD OF THE CABBALAH

The quest for the nearness of God which inspired the Jewish Cabbalists, inspired their Christian disciples as well. But the Christian Cabbalah had goals of its own—to validate the distinctive doctrines of the church. They were particularly interested in a confirmation of the doctrine of the trinity. They were aided in this quest by the Cabbalistic doctrine of the *sefirot*. The introduction of a male and female principle in the expression of God's creative self suggested to Christians that it is possible to speak of God as "begetting" and "begotten." The Jewish and the Christian Cabbalah spoke differently, though both employed the same language.

What permanent significance may be assigned to the rise of the Cabbalah in Judaism? Jewish mysticism has occasionally been presented as a response to the persecutions suffered by the Jewish people, especially the expulsion from Spain. Its final development into *hasidism* has likewise been explained as the reaction to the massacres of Polish Jewish communities by the bands of the "pogromist," Chmielnicki. It is significant, however, that some of the greatest exponents of Jewish mysticism, including the creators of the *Zohar* literature, did their work during the golden age of Jewish life in Spain. The rise of the Cabbalah among the Jews of Poland occurred likewise during the period of greatest prosperity in Polish Jewry. It is significant, too, that the growth of mysticism among the Jews, as we have noted previously, was paralleled by a like development in the Christian community. Mysticism is more than a by-product of social conditions. Mysticism, like rationalism, represents a permanent expression of the human spirit to orient itself to the world, and to find an answer to the ultimate questions about human existence.

The mystical way has had its adherents throughout the history of human thought. In its essential elements, it is imposingly expounded in the theories of neo-Platonism. Its most recent spokesman in modern thought has been Henri Bergson. The events through which men have passed have undoubtedly influenced their choice of a philosophy of life, but ideas have their own cogency. The modern student of culture must weigh the ideas of the mystics as well as of the rationalists on their own merits, and not merely as historically conditional responses to problems that have passed with the passing of an age.

The Cabbalah in its many ramifications, represents an important treasury of Jewish wisdom. It is not all of one order, of course. The many different exponents of the Cabbalah shared a common quest for the nearness of God, and they employed a similar vocabulary in expressing some of their basic conceptions. Yet they were free to look at religion and life from the unique perspectives of their own minds. And the vast literature of the Cabbalah is often differentiated in its teachings, reflecting the differentiated minds of its creators.

The modern reader is often baffled by the Cabbalah. Its language abounds in all kinds of strange imagery. Its flights from reality, its visions and revelations about things earthly as well as divine often leave the modern reader in bewilderment. Its authentic ideas are all too often obscured by hyperbole and exaggeration. The Cabbalah was stripped of much of its exaggerations in its hasidic transformation. It is in *hasidism* that Jewish mysticism re-establishes its contact with reality, and takes as its goal the hallowing of life, not its transcendence.

An important figure who helped pave the way for this transformation was Rabbi Judah Loew of Prague (1512-1609), who is the subject of our present study.

II
A Portrait of the Master

Chapter 1

THE ORIGIN OF RABBI JUDAH

IN THE YEAR 1584, on the Sabbath between the New Year and the Day of Atonement, which is celebrated in Judaism as the Sabbath of Repentance, there stood in the pulpit of the principal synagogue of the Bohemian capital city, Prague, the venerable Rabbi Judah Loew. He was tall and distinguished looking. The moment was dramatic because it was a prelude to a great decision. The chief rabbi of the city, Isaac Melling, had died. Judah Loew, a brilliant thinker and one of the most renowned scholars in medieval Jewry, was the logical person to succeed him in office. A large assemblage of people, including the members of the all-powerful community council, listened attentively.

Rabbi Loew spoke of the dignity of man, of his central position in the hierarchy of existence. But he reminded his listeners that man may forfeit his dignity by living meanly. He denounced the envy which makes men begrudge their neighbor's good fortune. He denounced the evils of sensuous living, of making the indulgence of the palate a major goal in one's existence. Above all, he denounced the prevalent vice of slander, which will unhesitatingly assail character and make light of the reputations of other people. Through these vices men alienate themselves from God and destroy what should be the chief glory of their lives.

He directed himself especially to the calumny which was then being circulated throughout Europe and which reflected on the honor of a number of leading Jewish families who were called by the derisive epithet "nadler," a term suggesting illegitimate birth in the middle high-German dialect. Then

FROM THE WORLD OF THE CABBALAH

he summoned ten leading citizens to come to the pulpit with scrolls of the Torah in their hands and he intoned the solemn formula of excommunication against the slanderers. The address was memorable, and it revealed the full stature of Rabbi Loew, his depth of feeling as well as his moral courage.

A short time thereafter some of these same men who had listened to Rabbi Loew met in another assembly. They were gathered to elect the chief rabbi. When the vote was finally cast it proved to be in favor of Rabbi Loew's brother-in-law, Rabbi Isaac Hayot. Rabbi Loew missed one of his life's ambitions and the leaders of Prague Jewry missed covering their community with glory. Yet the results should have surprised no one.[1]

The personal life of Rabbi Judah remains shrouded in obscurity.

A prolific writer, he yet tells little about himself. In unguarded moments he offers us occasional personal notes, and they shed invaluable light on his life and his times. These notes are, however, very few. His gaze is consistently turned outward, toward the world which he sought to influence, toward the ideas which he endeavored to expound. His own eventful life received but faint attention from his pen. Our principal sources of knowledge about him are indirect—occasional comments by contemporaries, a tombstone inscription, which extols his many-sided accomplishments, and family chronicles in which an oral tradition is reduced to writing for the benefit of posterity.[2]

Judah was born in 1512 to a distinguished Jewish family which hailed from the German city of Worms but which was now settled in Posen, Poland. The Loew family had apparently left Germany to escape anti-Jewish persecutions for which the German people seem to have had an affinity even in those days. Poland was more tolerant, and a stream of Jewish refugees had come to make their homes there.

Judah came into a home where scholarship was a normal goal for a young boy. His father, Bezalel, was a learned man.

FROM THE WORLD OF THE CABBALAH

His three older brothers, Hayim, Sinai and Samson were all distinguished scholars who participated in the rabbinic and philosophic discussions of their time. Judah's development was within the pattern of his own family circle.

Judah's education began along conventional lines. At an early age, he was introduced to the study of the Talmud. In itself a formidable discipline, Talmudic study was then encumbered with all kinds of commentaries and super-commentaries. And the pedagogy of the time relished in the cultivation of dialectical skill by subjecting every Talmudic text to minute analysis, whose triumph was the discovery of contradictions which were then to be removed in brilliant feats of reconciliation. Judah was later to break with this kind of pedagogy and he proclaimed a holy war against the sterility of current education, with its emphasis on "pilpul," as the prevalent method of Talmud study was called. At first, he accepted it, however, and he became quite a skillful dialectitian, a master of Talmudic knowledge, even by the official standards of the dominant academicians.[3]

He studied the Zohar, the Bible of the Cabbalists, zealously, as well as the rest of that esoteric literature. Whereas the Talmud said very little, at least not directly, about God and how we were to find a way to Him, here he found a continued preoccupation with the very questions which stirred him most, questions about man and his destiny, questions about God Who was both hidden and near, beyond the universe, and yet the very breath of its being. A poetic glow, suffused with warmth and the romance of deep faith was distilled by the Cabbalistic writings. They struck a responsive chord in the imaginative Judah.

Judah supplemented his education with avid reading in all other branches of Jewish knowledge. He was a master of Biblical study, with the great commentaries of Rashi, Nahmanides, ibn Ezra, Kimhi and Gersonides. He read the great classics in Jewish philosophy, the writings of Maimonides, Albo, and Crescas. He had an equally imposing command of the secular knowledge of his time. He was familiar with the teachings of the Greek philosophers, and with the current knowledge of physics, mathematics and astronomy. His mind was open to the world. His writings which were to appear later on, show that nothing missed his versatile mind. He alludes to the popular historical work, Josippon, to the new astronomy of Copernicus, to the discovery of America, and to Luther's translation of the Bible into German.[4]

Rabbi Judah does not mention any teachers under whom he studies. His break with the conventional curriculum is undoubtedly responsible for this. He could not refer to his teachers in praise, and he would not refer to them in blame. But much of Judah's scholarship was undoubtedly the result of his own intellectual labors. His wide erudition and the originality of his ideas reveal him as an independent mind, who did not depend on others to chart a path for him.[5]

Rabbi Judah's marriage to his wife Pearl, has been surrounded by the Loew family chronicler, Meir Perles, with romance. The bride's father, a well known Prague merchant called "Shmelke" (a corruption for Samuel), suffered business reverses shortly after the couple was engaged. Thus he could not meet the terms of the financial arrangements in favor of the young couple, as had been stipulated. Thereupon he offered to cancel the engagement. Judah, however, was not interested in the financial settlement and he persisted in his love for Pearl. There was a long delay in the wedding, while the bride established herself in a bakery shop in order to help support the family. The marriage finally occurred in 1544. Bride and groom, according to the same chronicler, were then 32 and 28 years old respectively.[6]

Their marriage was a very happy one, and they were blessed with seven children, six daughters and a son. All six daughters married into prominent Prague families. His son, Bezalel, became rabbi in Cologne, Germany, where he headed a rabbini-

FROM THE WORLD OF THE CABBALAH

cal academy. Rabbi Judah was deeply grieved when this son met an untimely death in 1600.[7] Rabbi Judah's public career took him to many parts of Central and Eastern Europe but his heart was always in Prague, the home of his wife's family and of his own children.

Chapter 2

THE CULTURE OF THE SIXTEENTH CENTURY

Rabbi Judah's career can best be appreciated against the background of the times in which he lived. The sixteenth century was an age of great movement and change. The growth of cities and the rise of a middle class of merchants, financiers and manufacturers, proved a revolutionary force in the medieval world. It spelled the breakdown of feudalism. The destruction of the social equilibrium based on feudalism released a new struggle for position among the different social classes in Europe. Kings, princes, peasants, and cities, as the centers of the new middle class of merchants—all struggled for the assertion of their "rights" in the emergent pattern of a new social order. The physical confines of the medieval world were broken by the daring explorers and seamen who opened up for European colonization and exploitation the vast new world across the Atlantic. The advances in science, culminating in the revolutionary theory of Copernicus that the earth was but a tiny planet moving round the sun, changed man's conception of the universe itself, revealing it as far more complex and mysterious than had been assumed in the past.

The cultural expression of these changes was the Renaissance and its concomitant movement, humanism. Both those movements reflected a spirit of worldliness, a preoccupation with nature, with the fulfillments of mundane life, rather than with the values of an other-worldly existence. They reflected a new sense of the dignity of the individual. All these were aided by the diffusion of knowledge and of new ideas as a result of the perfection of the printing press. The first printing press was set up in the middle of the 15th century. By 1500 there were in Europe, according to one estimate, at least a million books of thirty thousand titles, and over a thousand printers.

One of the by-products of these developments was a rising trend toward mysticism. The political and religious instabilities of the time and the collapse of the familiar conception of the universe undermined man's sense of personal security. Thus there was stimulated a new interest in mysticism, in the quest for God as an object of personal experience, rather than of dogmatic knowledge. A reflection of this trend was the gradual replacement of the philosophy of Aristotle which had extolled reason by that of Plato, whose thinking showed a greater affinity for mystical experience.

Mysticism was partly speculative and partly "practical." On the speculative side mysticism endeavored to explain the workings of God in creation, in terms close to man's experience. The "practical" side of mysticism tended to degenerate to magic. Conceiving the world as governed by a hierarchy of divine forces, in which the higher command and the lower obey, the mystic sought to unite himself with the higher realm, through secret rites, especially through the invocation of the secret name of God. It was the theory of "practical" mysticism that through his union with the higher realm the mystic was in a position to draw upon its power in order to control the realm below. The effort to control nature led many of the "practical" mystics to alchemy which flourished in the 16th century. Abounding in all kinds of vagaries and superstitions, alchemy was nevertheless an important step toward the development of modern science. For it was rooted in the conviction that nature was in a sense an unfinished enterprise, waiting for man to learn her laws and to adapt her to his own needs.

It was inevitable that these revolutionary developments clash against the political and religious structure within which feudal Europe had been organized. The old medieval ideal of a world community expressed on the political plane in the Holy Roman Empire and, on the religious plane, in the Catholic Church, was shaken by the emergence of national states and national churches. For the new order meant differentiated group experiences in social, economic and cultural life, and the differentiation corresponded more or less to those vaguely defined territorial and ethnic units which dotted the map of Europe and which had been formed by the convergence of geographic and historic forces. More and more, the Holy Roman Empire became defunct, as national communities, corresponding to these differentiated group experiences, asserted themselves. And the same pressures, on the religious level, led to the rise of Protestantism, bringing religion also within the frame of national rather than supra-national organization.[8]

What was the Jewish situation at the turn of the sixteenth century? The social structure of the Middle Ages had assigned to the Jews a distinct existence. They were outside the feudal hierarchy which was based on land as the principal means for the production of wealth. The Jew played the part of the otherwise non-existent middle class. While Jews engaged in various handicrafts, one sector of the economy of Europe seemed to be largely in their hands—they were the merchants and the money lenders. The Jewish community maintained an autonomous existence within the larger Christian world. The Jews regulated their own social, economic and cultural affairs. They levied and collected their own taxes for the maintenance of their own institutions and for the payment of a general assessment to the state.

The state had ulterior motives in recognizing Jewish autonomy. For it facilitated the collection of taxes, which were levied against the Jewish community as a whole. As a means of strengthening its control over the Jewish community, the government occasionally interfered with elections to Jewish communal offices. In some instances, it did not hesitate to impose its favorite candidates on the community. Venal men can always be found who for personal gain will be willing to make common cause with their people's oppressors. In some instances, however, such appointees were given no choice; they had to take office under duress.

FROM THE WORLD OF THE CABBALAH

The Jews were subject to a great antipathy on the part of the Christian population surrounding them. The antipathy toward the Jew stemmed from the normal tensions which a rural population feels toward an urban population, toward the merchants who appear as the "profiteers" in the various transactions of the market, and especially toward the money lenders who were accused of charging exorbitant rates of interest. The Jews were resented also because they were the only element of heterogeneity in an otherwise homogeneous population. The Jews, moreover, were not only different. In the culture of the dominant religion, they were branded with harsh terms; they were represented as the villains in the drama of man's salvation. Christian theology referred to them as the "Christ-killers," who were to suffer because they had rejected the "saviour."

The cultural transformation initiated during the 16th century seemed to offer the Jews redress from their hardships. The disabilities of the Jews were part of the old world order which was being challenged everywhere, and if there was to be a reformation in Europe, was not the condition of the Jewish group to be included in the benefits of the new dispensation? The leading spirits of the new age, moreover, had shown a marked interest in Jewish culture. They included Hebrew in the classical heritage which they sought to recover for their own day. Under the tutelage of Jewish scholars, Christian Hebraists studied not only the Hebrew language but also the Hebrew commentators on Scripture. They studied with special zeal the writing of Jewish mysticism, the Cabbalah, in which they found guidance for their own brooding spirits. A day of better understanding between Judaism and Christianity seemed at last to have dawned upon the world.

As the sixteenth century continued to unfold, however, this hope was soon frustrated. The development of Hebraic tendencies among the Christian humanists was resented by the spokesmen of conventional Christianity. Thus Johannes Forster (1495-1556), in the preface to his Hebrew Dictionary, de-

FROM THE WORLD OF THE CABBALAH

nounced the dependence of the humanists on Jewish scholarship: "Often I have wondered about the feeblemindedness of my Christian colleagues who without any discernment have embraced the commentaries of the Jews in which there is no light, no knowledge of God, no spirit. . . . They (the Jews) do not discern and see that the end of the Law is the Son of God. . . . Therefore their dictionaries and commentaries have brought more obscurity and error into the church of Christ than light and truth. . . ." Even a man like Erasmus criticized the trend to Hebraism and wrote disparagingly of Jews as well as of Judaism: "The Jewish race is fed full of lifeless tales and produces nothing but a little vapor, to wit the Cabbalah, the Talmud, the Tetragrammaton, the Gates of Light, and such vain titles. . . . Would that the Christian Church did not rely so much on the Old Testament. . . ."

The wars between Catholic orthodoxy and Protestant heresy also had a detrimental effect on the Jewish group. The defenders of the Catholic Church charged the rising Protestant sects with being a "Judaizing" heresy. In self-defense, the spokesmen of Catholicism thus tended to take a more hostile attitude toward the influence of Judaism. Protestantism, at the same time, to disprove the charge, accentuated its own polemic against the Jews. From both divisions of Christendom, there emanated a persistent and aggressive propaganda against Judaism.

The social and political forces of the new age likewise reacted against the Jewish group. The rise of cities and the development of a native middle class added the pressure of business competition against the Jews. The movement toward nationalism also proved a source of anti-Jewish hostility, for the Jews were looked upon as an "alien" cultural element that was guilty of disturbing the inner unity of the new society. There was some abatement of mob violence against the Jews in the sixteenth century, but they became increasingly subject to expulsions. The great expulsion from Spain in 1492 was followed by a series of expulsions from the various other European states throughout the sixteenth century. As one historian put it, "Mere segregation, prescribed by the Church, and fanatical massacres were succeeded by systematic expulsion in the interests of national uniformity in the several states—a symptom of a new exclusive force—nationality." [9]

CHAPTER 3

JEWISH LIFE IN BOHEMIA AND POLAND

RABBI JUDAH'S career was centered in Bohemia and in Poland. We do not know the precise date of the earliest Jewish settlements in Bohemia. There are references to Bohemian Jewish merchants which go back to the beginnings of the tenth century. The first and most important city where the Jews settled was the Bohemian capital, Prague. Toward the end of the fourteenth century it has been estimated that some three thousand Jewish inhabitants resided in Prague. The annals of Bohemian Jewry in the Middle Ages reflect both incidents of freedom and prosperity and, at the same time, the pressure of growing hostility on the part of the Christian population. The Jews pursued a variety of occupations. The records portray them as farmers, weavers, miners, masons, sailors, musicians, in addition to merchants, and money lenders. The Jews were an important factor in the trade with the interior of Austria, Bavaria and Saxony. A Jew, Mordecai Meisel, handled all the financial transactions of the imperial household. He grew to be one of the wealthiest men in the empire, and he was a confidant of the imperial family. He was a great benefactor of the Jewish community, using his wide influence in the imperial court on behalf of his people.

The forces of hostility were, however, also at work to undermine the position of Bohemian Jewry. The war between Catholicism and Protestantism filled the atmosphere with the usual charges and counter-charges in which Judaism was presented as the great enemy of Christendom. Thus when John Huss was burnt for his heresies, his accusers heaped upon him the charge: "O thou accursed Judas who, breaking away from the counsels of peace, hast taken counsel with the Jews.'

FROM THE WORLD OF THE CABBALAH

In 1526 Bohemia became part of the Holy Roman Empire, and thus within the main orbit of the Reformation emanating from Germany. The pressures against Jews were now intensified, finally leading to a series of expulsions, which were, however, soon followed by an invitation to return. They were expelled and readmitted in 1542, 1557 and 1571. In a sermon which Rabbi Judah preached in 1573, he compared these expulsions and invitations of return to the actions of fickle lovers, who unite and separate as the impulse moves them.

Polish Jewry was subject to a similar development. During the early middle ages, Poland was a haven of refuge for the Jews. An economically backward area, Poland depended on the Jewish group to fill a serious gap in its economy—the lack of a native middle class. The Jews occupied themselves with land tenure, farming, manufacture. They held concessions to tolls and excise taxes, to crown lands and princely states. They worked salt mines, traded in lumber and exported grain. At the beginning of the century when Rabbi Judah was born, Poland had a rapidly growing Jewish population, and in actual numbers it was in excess of 50,000. By the end of that century it reached a half million souls.

But here too there were forces at work against the Jewish community. The king and the upper layers of the nobility, who were dependent on the Jewish middlemen economically, stood by to guard their rights and to protect them against hostile pressures. That pressure came from the lower order of the nobility who were eager to displace the Jews in urban careers and from the native merchants in the large cities who resented the Jews as competitors. It also came from Church circles, as a phase of the feuds between the adherents of the Reformation and its adversaries.

The pressure of anti-Jewish influence led to local incidents in which Jews suffered violence. Occasionally the royal protection relaxed and the cities, acting upon the inspiration of native merchants, were able to enforce restrictive legislation against the Jewish population. In 1520 the Jewish merchants of Posen were forbidden to maintain stores in the market place outside their own quarter in the city. In 1523 they were limited in their rights of domicile, being restricted to specific quarters. A prohibition was also issued against new Jewish settlers entering the city.

An event which must have made a deep impression on the Jews in Rabbi Judah's time was the martyrdom of Catherine Zaleshovska, the wife of a city alderman in nearby Cracow in 1539. Catherine had come under anti-trinitarian influences, and at the age of 80 was charged by church authorities with being a secret adherent of Judaism. They questioned her concerning her faith, and stubbornly she defended the contention that "God could not be born as a human being." A contemporary chronicler continues his report of the incident: "When it was not possible to detach her from her Jewish beliefs, it was decided to convict her of blasphemy. She was taken to the city jail and a few days later burned. She went to her death without the slightest fear." This event was followed by searches upon Jews in order to uncover the details of the "Judaizing" conspiracy.[10]

The problems which confronted the Jewish communities in Bohemia and Poland and with which Rabbi Judah was called on to deal derived in part from the pressures of the outside world and in part from their own internal weaknesses.

There were a variety of forces at work to weaken the Jewish community internally, at the very time when it was called on to play so crucial a role in the struggle of the Jew for survival. For one thing, an intellectual ferment was at work in Jewry that seriously menaced its way of life. There was the problem of rationalism, emanating principally from the writing of Maimonides, which seemed to many a dangerous influence calculated to undermine the religious loyalties of the people. Especially as interpreted by his later disciples, Maimonides seemed to stand for a revolutionary reinterpretation of Jewish tradition, in which some of the most cherished beliefs of the common people were repudiated. It had been noticed also, that in time of testing, when men were called to validate their faith by the ready acceptance of exile or martyrdom, it was the common people who showed the greatest steadfastness, while those who had pursued a philosophic education often betrayed their faith.

There was also a new source of challenge to religion in the new science which had arisen in the sixteenth century. The leading representatives of the new science, men such as Pomponazzi, Copernicus, Bruno, Bacon, Brahe and Galileo repudiated doctrines which had been held indispensable by all religious communities. Pomponazzi (1462-1525) denied the possibility of proving the immortality of the soul, miracles, or free will, and he died without the consolation of the church. Copernicus (1473-1543) undermined the traditional conception of the universe, based on Aristotle. In his astronomical system, our earth is robbed of its centrality; it becomes a humble member in a vast planetary system. As the earth was humbled, so was man, its central character. And how could man then pose as the center of all creation, as the Bible described him? Bruno (1548-1600), the exponent of the philosophical implications of Copernicus, denied divine providence over the lives of individuals; he rejected the belief in miracles; and he questioned the efficacy of prayer. He was burnt at the stake as a heretic after seven years of imprisonment. In Francis Bacon (1561-1639), Tycho Brahe (1546-1601), and Galileo (1564-1641), science is not only exemplified in new theory, but the method of observation, and experimentation is held out as the indispensable path to truth. The conflict between religion and science was waged principally in the Christian community, but its impact was felt among the Jews as well.

There were some in the Jewish community who responded with a holy war against science and philosophy. For the philosophic and scientific mind seemed to them a menace, a source of influence that would undermine their very existence as a community in medieval civilization. Thus in 1559 Rabbi Aaron of Posen preached a sermon in the principal synagogue of the city in which he denounced all secular studies, and he singled out Maimonides for special censure, as a pillar of heresy. He demanded complete absorption in the study of the Talmud, objecting even to the study of Bible. He only echoed a mood that was gaining headway in Jewish communities, especially in Central and Eastern Europe. But was not obscurantism equally dangerous to the survival of the Jews? Could one meet the challenge of reason by closing one's mind and building barricades against the spirit's straying in forbidden paths?[11]

The Jewish community was also troubled by the problem of assimilation. Despite formal animosity between the Jewish and Christian communities, there were many instances of individuals crossing the frontiers and joining in intimate expressions of mutual friendliness. Especially in Bohemia was this tendency noticeable. The every-day language of the Bohemian Jews was Czech. An official register of Prague Jewry, dated 1546, shows that many of them had adopted Czech names. The tendency developed also for the Bohemian Jews to shed some of their old customs which had made for separatism between Jews and Christians, as is indicated in the widespread disregard of the old ban against non-Jewish wine.

According to Talmudic sources wine handled by non-Jews was to be shunned. This ban was part of the Talmudists' struggle against the idolatrous cults prevalent in their day, since wine was commonly used as libations to idols. Wine was also banned as a means of discouraging social contact between the Jewish and pagan communities and thereby to prevent inter-marriages between members of the two groups. In Bohemian and German communities there developed a movement to regard this old prohibition as obsolete, since Christians were not considered idolators and intermarriage was not a prevalent problem. This movement was, of course, aided by the fact that in Bohemia wine was a common article of diet, normally taken with each meal, and it was therefore difficult to draw the line between one kind of wine and another. The Bohemian rabbinate was apparently impressed with the attitude of the people and acquiesced in this growing laxity. But could the Jewish community maintain itself if those invisible walls of custom and law insulating, and to that extent safeguarding it, were to break down? Friendly relations with the outside world were desirable, but was there not danger in assimilation? In an age when the Jewish community had to fight for its life, could it afford to shed even a part of its protective armor?

The internal decadence which threatened the Jewish community derived also from certain abuses characterizing its organizational life. This was especially evident in Bohemia, with its great center of Jewish life in Prague. The community suffered from internal dissension, which was created in part by its heterogeneous population. In addition to native Bohemians, there also settled in Prague Jewish exiles from Spain and immigrants from Italy, Germany, France, Poland, Turkey and Palestine. They were, no doubt, attracted by the larger opportunities in this great metropolis of Central Europe, but the differences between them often led to misunderstanding and conflict.

Prague Jewry was also troubled by an oligarchy which ruled its communal life. Its board of community elders represented all Bohemian Jewry before the government. They apportioned and collected taxes. They appointed rabbis and judges. But the real power was always in the hands of the few wealthy families. For according to prevailing custom, the proportionate contribution in taxes was the yardstick for determining power in the affairs of the community. Under these circumstances, officials, religious as well as civil, became mere puppets in the hands of the representatives of entrenched wealth.

This condition was further aggravated by the regulation calling for frequent elections of rabbis and judges, which made these men subservient to those upon whose favor they depended for a renewal of stay in their positions. An imperial edict, dated 1580, confirmed the rule of annual elections for Jewish community officials in Prague. It even demanded a unanimous vote to certify an election! The authority of those serving on the electing body was thus made absolute, to the detriment of any independence on the part of those chosen to administer the institutions of the Jewish community.

The most serious abuse was in the prevailing system of education. In Poland as well as Bohemia, the schools concentrated on the study of the Talmud with its commentaries and super-commentaries. All other elements in the rich culture of Judaism were ignored. Even the Bible and the Hebrew language were neglected. The goal of those schools was to produce dialecticians who could argue brilliantly the fine points of a Talmudic text. The Jewish schools paralleled fully the pedagogy current in the middle ages generally, which was beset with a mania for disputation, fine-spun analysis and argumentation. The decadence of the Jewish schools was fully reflected in the men they raised. The rabbis trained in those schools preached sermons that were not directed at the simple exposition of doctrine or the elucidation of some problem in life. They revelled instead in the clever use of Scriptural verses, which they often took out of context. The academicians as well as the pulpiteers suffered from the same distorted goal which extolled sophistry above the sincere quest for truth, and which reduced Judaism to a caricature of its real self.[12]

These were staggering problems with which the Jewish community was called on to deal. The man who understood these problems and sought to chart the way for their solution was Rabbi Judah.

Chapter 4

CONFLICT AND ACHIEVEMENT

RABBI JUDAH endeavored to deal with all the formidable problems facing medieval Jewry in his work as rabbi and communal leader, and especially in his writings. His long and eventful ministry began in the city of Nicolsberg, where he served as rabbi of the province of Moravia. He assumed that post in 1553 and remained there for twenty years, till 1573.

Only faint echoes of his ministry at Nicolsberg have come down to us. He endeavored to bring order in Moravian community affairs. He edited a collection of various community ordinances which had been promulgated by earlier authorities, to which he added some of his own. These ordinances deal with various current community problems, including education, elections to community offices, and methods of taxation. They seek to improve the moral conditions of the people, and they speak out specifically against ostentation in dress among the Jewish population. In 1572 Rabbi Judah presided at a meeting of a council of Moravian Jewish representatives which dealt with various problems facing the Jewish group. Rabbi Judah fought for decorum at religious services, battling particularly against the widespread practice of conversation during prayer. He added a special prayer to the synagogue liturgy in denunciation of Jews who for reasons of personal gain collaborated with the government in oppressive measures against the Jewish group. Years after he had left his post as provincial rabbi of Moravia, he was approached by the Jews of Prausnitz, a city in Moravia, to arrange for them a body of regulations to govern their communal life.

We do not know the precise circumstances which led to the termination of Rabbi Judah's stay in Nicolsberg. Perhaps it

FROM THE WORLD OF THE CABBALAH

was due to the general deterioration in the conditions of Moravian Jewry. As the contemporary chronicler David Ganz reports it: "This was a time of mourning and persecution for the Jews of Moravia, and many gave their lives as martyrs, in sanctification of God's name. They died by fire and sword, until at last the great and noble King Maximilian II intervened on behalf of those who were being persecuted without cause . . . and in 1574 he put an end to this period of suffering." Rabbi Judah's departure from Nicolsberg thus coincided with a period of demoralization in Moravian Jewry. It may well be that he changed his residence in order to find a freer atmosphere for his labors.

Rabbi Judah left Nicolsberg to settle in Prague. It is significant, however, that he came to Prague in an unofficial capacity. He had not been invited to become the city's rabbi. What drew Rabbi Judah to Prague under such circumstances? The records shed little light on the subject; and we are left to conjecture. There were, of course, family considerations that must have weighed heavily with Rabbi Judah. His wife's family resided in Prague, as did his children. Being an independently wealthy man, he was not deterred by the fact that he would reside in Prague without an official position to offer him remuneration for his services. He surely did not need formal designation as rabbi of the community to allow him to assert his leadership as a teacher of the Torah and as a zealous guardian of its principles in their bearing upon human life. The ultimate authority behind a rabbi's leadership derives from the fact of his ordination, and not from the action of laymen who may elect him to a particular rabbinic office.

Rabbi Judah's attraction for Prague must also have been inspired by the city's preeminence as a great cultural center of Judaism. The culture of Prague Jewry had a long tradition behind it. In the early 15th century three famous rabbis had their posts in Prague: Menahem Karo, his half-brother Abigdor, and Yom Tob Lippman Muehlhausen. Rabbi Menahem was a student of philosophy and he wrote a commentary on the Maimonidean classic, *The Guide to the Perplexed*, as well as on several other philosophic texts. Rabbi Abigdor was a poet, a Cabbalist, and a staunch defender of his people and his faith against the calumnies of Christian polemicists. Rabbi Yom Tob Muehlhausen has left his permanent mark on the history of Jewish thought. He wrote on philosophy and Cabbalah, and he composed liturgical hymns. He was a frequent disputant on behalf of Judaism in the religious polemics of the times. He debated with learned Christian priests and with apostate Jews, who sought to demonstrate loyalty to their new faith by slandering the old. His *Nizahon* (Victory), is a record of these disputations, and it offers a fine analysis of the points at issue between Judaism and Christianity. The first Hebrew printing press was established in Prague in 1512, a clear indication of an advanced cultural life in Prague Jewry.

A chronicler writing in 1604 extols Prague as a great center of Jewish life. "In Prague," he writes, "there exists a very famous community, whose fragrance is widely spread; a big town, full of wise, learned men, rich men, all adorned with the crown of a good reputation. They are distinguished by knowledge of Torah, piety and the fear of God; a holy community for which it would be vain to seek an equal and the like of which has seldom been found."

In Prague, Rabbi Judah opened an academy for higher Jewish studies, and for eleven years he carried on his work in an unofficial capacity. The academy opened by Rabbi Judah was something novel in rabbinic education. It was dedicated to the study of Torah as an end in itself. It offered no ordinations. It invited advanced students to deepen their knowledge of Judaism, with no thought of utilitarian considerations.

The method and content of study, moreover, reflected his own general theories of what constituted true culture. He avoided the over-concentrations on the study of Talmud, offering instead a broad education in all branches of Jewish learning. Among his disciples was David Ganz, the famous historian, mathematician and astronomer. Another of his disciples was Yom Tob Lippman Heller, a man of wide erudition in all branches of secular as well as sacred knowledge, whose best known work is his very lucid commentary on the Mishnah, *Tosefot Yom Tob*. These and a number of other men reflect, by their own interests, the broad culture which they imbibed from their famous master.

Rabbi Judah also busied himself with the larger life of the Prague community. He helped set in order the affairs of the local burial society, and he helped establish popular societies for the study of Mishnah. He issued an edict against Jews who betrayed their own people by collaborating with the government's oppressive measures against them. He was the confidant and adviser of Mordecai Meisel who was the outstanding lay leader of Bohemian Jewry, especially in relations with municipal and imperial officials.

In 1583, as we noted previously, an opportunity came for Rabbi Judah to be elected chief rabbi of Prague. Rabbi Isaac Melling, the incumbent in the office of the Prague rabbinate, died. Rabbi Judah was invited to preach the sermon on the Sabbath of Repentance in the city's principal synagogue. He was the logical candidate for the office of chief rabbi. However, when election time came, he was passed by, in favor of his brother-in-law, Isaac Hayot.

The rejection of Rabbi Judah by the community leaders in Prague is not indicated in the sources, but it is not difficult to surmise the reasons for it. Ever since he had come to Prague, Rabbi Judah became a controversial figure in the community. A great scholar, an original thinker and at the same time a forceful personality, he clearly over-shadowed chief rabbi Isaac Melling. The latter continued his work in the city's leading synagogue, the Altneuschul, but the recently constructed Klaus synagogue, built with the help of Rabbi Judah's friend, the banker Mordecai Meisel, in honor of the emperor's friendly visit in the Jewish Ghetto in 1571, was made available to Rabbi Judah. People were quick to sense Rabbi Judah's superiority and they came to look to him for leadership. The re-organization of the community's burial society, for instance, was entrusted to him rather than to the chief rabbi. Isaac Melling represented the authority of the organized community and its lay leadership, and it was the official community and its leadership that felt itself challenged by Rabbi Judah's rise to popularity.

Rabbi Judah, moreover, committed another offense in the eyes of the ruling circles of Prague Jewry. He spoke his mind freely on all current problems and he did not hesitate to point the finger at the abuses which he saw rampant about him. Many of these abuses centered in the corruption of Jewish community government. Rabbi Judah had, in other words, attacked the very men whose voice was decisive in choosing the chief rabbi.

Rabbi Judah denounced the ruling circles of his community for wielding power selfishly. They oppressed the people by denying their workers an equitable wage, he charged, and by shifting tax burdens on those less able to carry them. He denounced the ignorant and corrupt judges who were named to office because of their wealth. The custom of designating one of the community elders as "primus" or "chief" was for him a perversion of the principle of equality which he wanted to prevail in all walks of life.

In some communities men of integrity and noble spirit exercised authority, but how different was the case in other communities, he lamented. "In some countries, and in some communities, they turn justice to wormwood. They have set up ignorant men as authorities, men who know not the meaning of justice and law. It has reached a point where those who are qualified, the real scholars, see with their own eyes the perversion of justice . . . and they are helpless even in redressing the cause of an orphan or a widow. . . . The true sages have no opportunity to correct the evil conditions of this generation, for those in power tell them 'you are not our *Ab Bet Din* (Head of the court of law) that we need be obliged to listen to you.' It is indeed more difficult to bear their yoke than the yoke of the gentiles. For when they sense that there be one who does not respect them and does not want to recognize their authority, they seek to subdue and oppress and persecute him with every kind of persecution. . . . Yet I say that one who fears the Lord must take heed unto himself not to stand before such men in judgment. . . . For whoever brings a case for judgment before a judge who was appointed only because of his wealth sets up idols of silver and idols of gold in place of God. . . . It is indeed a virtuous deed to show contempt for such men. The hands of Esau ordained them."

The rabbinate, he charged, was incapable of raising the moral level of the community because the rabbis were caught in the same vicious circle. The same men of wealth control the elections of the rabbi and they necessarily influence his utterances. The rabbi holding office in these communities, he wrote, is "dependent upon the men in authority and upon select individuals in the community. Every year or every three years they re-engage him to his position. And how can he help being afraid of them upon whom he is dependent? They may not retain him in his post."

Under such circumstances, the rabbinate necessarily becomes impotent. "If the scholars did not depend for their livelihood on them, the cause of the Torah would be advanced. They would surely reprove the people, as the failures of the people are their responsibility and they would not be subservient. But now, because they are dependent on them, every rabbi has a master over himself." Rabbi Judah records that the tension between the rabbis and lay leaders was a common feature of current community life. The laymen were suspicious of the rabbis and the rabbis were fearful of the laymen.

Rabbi Judah took the lay leaders to task for these conditions of the contemporary rabbinate. They caused the degradation of the rabbinate because they did not provide amply for the rabbi's needs, in accordance with the high dignity of his calling. Thus they made weaklings and beggars out of the rabbis. They acted as though "it was normal for scholars to be dependent on others and to be forced to ask for their support; and thereby they lowered the glory of the Torah to the very ground." Rabbi Judah extolled scholars who shun the professional rabbinate and achieve economic independence by engaging in various occupations, especially handicrafts, which offer one a sure livelihood. Thus they have earned their freedom, and they can then truly discharge their role as teachers of their people.

In the very sermon which he preached on that Sabbath of Repentance in 1584 and which was in a sense to serve as a "test," preliminary to the crucial election later on, Rabbi Judah stated his position in unmistaken language. It is the business of the ruler, he reminded his hearers, to attend to the needs of the poor and the lowly, rather than to serve the interests of the "great." For the cause of the poor is generally the just cause, and even the slightest deprivation of the poor is a deprivation of his very existence "since his livelihood depends on it."

On that same fateful Sabbath of Repentance, Rabbi Judah took occasion to make a public enactment of his edict of excommunication against those guilty of spreading the so-called "nadler" calumny. This was a very serious evil, and it had resulted in bringing untold anguish to countless Jewish families in Central Europe who were accused of illegitimacy. The departed were not spared, and they too were included in the slander. It would have set those families as pariahs in the Jewish community, and they had appealed for redress to the leading rabbis of the time. Rabbi Judah reports in the transcript of that memorable sermon how he met the issue. "This we did here in Prague on the Sabbath of Repentance in the year 1584," he writes. "We issued a mighty edict of excommunication in the presence of ten scrolls of the Torah which were held by the wise men of Prague, each a scroll in his hand, against the spread of any slander against the departed and against calling anyone in Israel by the slurring epithet of 'nadler.' "

FROM THE WORLD OF THE CABBALAH

Rabbi Judah showed himself a strong character, a man of passionate convictions, a crusader for a good cause. Such men become controversial figures. They invariably make enemies, especially among the men who wield power. Rabbi Judah's conduct on that Sabbath of Repentance was not calculated to ingratiate him with those whose consent was indispensable for the final decision as to the election of the chief rabbi.

There was also opposition in some circles to Rabbi Judah's theology. Rabbi Judah adopted the principal doctrines of the Cabbalah and tried to popularize them in his writings as well as his oral discourses. There were many who resented the inroads of the Cabbalah into the religious life of Jewry. Some of its doctrines seemed strange and bewildering. The Cabbalists generally kept their doctrine from the common people, and wrote only in hints and veiled allusions. Rabbi Judah's excursions into the Cabbalah show the usual reticence of the Cabbalist. Yet for those who could read between the lines his meanings were clear enough to be disturbing. Thus his emphasis on God's incomprehensibleness brought upon him the charge that he had made God totally unreal. It was voiced by no less an authority than the famous scholar Rabbi Eliezer Ashkenazi, and Rabbi Judah was forced to defend himself against the accusation.

Rabbi Judah also evoked fierce opposition with his insistence on the retention of the old law against non-Jewish wine. In his home community in Poland, that law remained in force and he saw no reason for its abrogation in Bohemia. He was not impressed with the arguments for abrogation. There were other institutions, he pointed out, which arose to meet needs that have passed, but that did not automatically nullify them. We have, for instance, the second day of each major Jewish festival, which was added during the time when the calendar was calculated by observing the positions of the new moon, to allow for possible delay in announcing the new calendar in Jewish communities in the diaspora. We now calculate the calendar mathematically and the old uncertainties are gone, but Jewish communities in the diaspora still add a second day to each of the major festivals.

Rabbi Judah's stand was also motivated by the special significance which the Cabbalah attached to the nature of wine. Hebrew letters have numerical equivalents and the numerical equivalent of the Hebrew word for wine, *yayin*, is 70, which is also the equivalent of the Hebrew word for secret or hidden, *sod*. This suggests the true quality of wine as something spiritual. The spiritual is the ultimate inner essence, surrounded by outer shells that must be penetrated. The ban against non-Jewish wine was therefore to be retained as symbolizing the necessity of safeguarding the spiritual essence of the Jewish people from encroachment by the spiritual essence of the non-Jewish communities.

Rabbi Judah wanted to take action against those violating the prohibition of non-Jewish wine, but the community leaders disputed his authority to do so. They told him bluntly: "You have no authority here and you have no competence in such matters." Years later, when he left Prague temporarily to assume the post of rabbi in Posen, he came out with an edict of excommunication directed not so much at the public that used this wine as against the rabbis that condoned it. He demanded the suspension of all rabbinic ordinations in Moravia. There the evil was the greatest, and the rabbis seemed to acquiesce in what the lay public was doing. The Moravian rabbinate was therefore untrustworthy, and Rabbi Judah actually proclaimed an edict of excommunication against any scholar, who would dare ordain as rabbi any one in Moravia, no matter how otherwise deserving. He conceded to only one exception—where a candidate for ordination could demonstrate that he had opposed the use of such wine through "the greater part of his life."

The terms of this edict were all-inclusive: "There is to be no ordination for residents of Moravia, whether in or outside their community, unless one knows the candidate and has ascertained that he has respected this prohibition through the greater part of his life." Rabbi Judah issued this edict, long after the elections in 1584, but this edict remains a striking commentary on the man and on the extent to which he was prepared to fight for his principles.

The opposition to Rabbi Judah must have derived finally from his attack on the popular Jewish culture of his time. He refused to respect institutions simply because convention had hallowed them. The popular hymn on God's unity, known as the *Shir ha-yihud* which was recited at the conclusion of the morning service, seemed to him a pretentious dissertation on a subject where man ought to show greater reticence, and he objected to it. It was not the work of scholars, but of laymen who imagined that through such expressions of piety they "would attain to the inner chamber." If it should prove impossible to break people away from this hymn, he explained, then it should at least be shifted to a less prominent part of the service.

Rabbi Judah objected to another equally hallowed prayer recited during the High Holiday season, the penitential hymn which begins with the words "makhnise rahamim haknisu rahamenu lifne baal ha-rahamim." This prayer pre-supposes the notion that angels act as mediators between man and God, and it turns to these mediators with the plea: "O, you who present man's plea for mercy, do you bring our pleas for mercy before the Author of Mercy." Rabbi Judah denounced this prayer because it implies that man may pray to beings other than God. His conception of piety demanded that man seek the divine source of mercy in a direct effort, invoking no intermediaries to aid in his quest. He suggested changing the text of the prayer, so as to remove the offensive implications.

Rabbi Judah's most radical attack was centered on the current tradition in the study of the Talmud. He denounced the rabbinic learning of his time, with its concentration on a curriculum of Talmudic dialectics, with its peak achievement in "pilpul." What was generally regarded as the mark of highest achievement in the knowledge of the Torah, he scorned as nothing but ostentation. He advocated a revolution in the schools, calling for a return to the study of Mishnah, and of Bible. He was especially concerned that study shall not be a refined play for the intellect, pursued for its own sake, but a means for building character, for illuminating the continuing religious needs and practices of the time. He berated the rabbis for their artificial sermons which delighted those interested in dialectics, but left the people without real spiritual guidance. In his day, these were novel ideas and they branded him a radical, an innovator.

It was not only Rabbi Judah's views that evoked opposition. It was also the vehemence with which he expounded them. Thus he spoke of the time when he himself had studied "pilpul" as his period of "madness" and "perversity," and he threatened those who continued to cling to the conventional methods of study with the ban. "Such men," he said, "should not be regarded as scholars, and whoever publicly flaunts his disrespect at them has done a praiseworthy deed." These and similar expressions show how keenly Rabbi Judah felt on the subject, but they also reflect a spirit that was not given too readily to the deft art of making friends among men of power and high station.

It is significant too that Rabbi Jacob Pollack, the popularizer of the study of "pilpul," had been rabbi in Prague for many years. He had undoubtedly made many friends among the educated circles in the community. Rabbi Judah's position was a direct challenge to them. He had thus arrayed against himself the leaders of culture as well as the leaders of wealth.

Rabbi Samuel Bachrach, who was married to a grand-daughter of Rabbi Judah, alludes to the fierce opposition Rabbi Judah had aroused among some of his contemporaries. "I am proud to remember," he wrote in a letter, "how they heaped upon our great master the vilest insults, all because of jealousy and hatred, though his piety had been recognized throughout the world."

It is pertinent to add that Rabbi Hayot who was preferred

for the position over Rabbi Judah, was a staunch exponent of "pilpul." The feelings engendered by the rivalry of the two men are clearly echoed in a comment by a grandson of Rabbi Judah. "I have never yet heard or read the praise of such hair-splitting," he writes, "as is offered by the learned Rabbi Isaac Hayot in the prefaces to his *P'ne Yitzhak* and *Pahad Yitzhak*. But everyone who reads the *Hiluk Biluk* (a term of derision for pilpul) printed in the preface of the aforementioned book will immediately recognize his grievous errors. May the Almighty protect us."

The full scope of Rabbi Judah's thinking could not have been known at the time of the elections for chief rabbi. His books, for the most part, had not yet appeared. But his first work *Gur Arye*, a study of Rashi's Biblical commentary, had been published in Prague in 1578, and there he already gave a general indication of the bent of his mind. Some of his sharpest criticism of the corrupt leadership of the community is voiced in this volume.

The opposition aroused by this work must have been profound. For his next volume, the *Geburot ha-Shem*, a study of divine providence in the early history of Israel, which was published in 1582, appeared anonymously and not in Prague but in Cracow. Rabbi Judah's caution did not, however, undo the damage. The record, if still incomplete, was nevertheless decisive, and it spoke against him. The willingness to conform is an important attribute in those who are ambitious for high office. Rabbi Judah was a non-conformist, and the leaders of Prague Jewry did not want him to be the city's chief rabbi.

The election of Rabbi Isaac Hayot made Rabbi Judah's position in Prague, even in an unofficial capacity, untenable. The situation could easily lend itself to controversy and create a rift in the family. There were other communities eager to win Rabbi Judah's leadership. Posen invited him to become its rabbi, and he accepted the call, remaining there till about 1588, when he once more returned to Prague. Rabbi Isaac Hayot had resigned his position, and Rabbi Judah once more felt free to resume his work in the city with which he was destined to be linked in history.

During his second stay in Prague, Rabbi Judah received a plea from the Jews of Moravia to protect them against a new outburst of slander against certain distinguished families, charging them with being descendants of an oedipus marriage. He joined a number of rabbis in issuing an edict of excommunication against those guilty of spreading this wholly unfounded charge. In 1589, he delivered the sermon in the Altneuschul Synagogue on the Sabbath before Passover. It was published the following year in Prague. In 1589, there also appeared his commentary on the ethical treatise *Abot*, under the title *Derek ha-Hayim* (The Way of Life).

The most dramatic event in which Rabbi Judah was involved during this period was his audience with the emperor. In February, 1592, he was invited for an audience by Emperor Rudolph II, and the two men remained closeted for a lengthy conference. We have no definite knowledge as to the subject of this conference. Legends abound, offering all kinds of elaboration upon the incident. The suggestion has been made that the emperor, who was a great student of alchemy, may have wanted to consult the famous rabbi who had won renown as a Cabbalist. It was in the Cabbalah that people in those days sought the answer to their interest in the occult. Another suggestion has been made that Rabbi Judah may have sought the audience, once and for all to expose before the emperor the libels which were being propagated against Jews, and which formed the basis of the mob violence as well as the oppressive legislation enacted against them. Perhaps Rabbi Judah's renown as a learned sage and great personality had reached the emperor who sought to satisfy his curiosity by means of this audience. Whatever the circumstances that led to this audience, it is a clear indication of Rabbi Judah's fame and of the recognition which had come to him as leader of the Jewish community.

Despite Rabbi Judah's widely recognized eminence, he was yet to be snubbed a second time by the officials of Prague

FROM THE WORLD OF THE CABBALAH

Jewry. In 1592 a new election was held for the office of chief rabbi. Again they ignored Rabbi Judah. They elected Rabbi Mordecai Jaffe. Thereupon Rabbi Judah left Prague once more, accepting for the second time a call to Posen, where he was to become chief rabbi of Poland. He remained in his new post for six years.

The records are meager as to his activities while rabbi in Poland. In 1592 on the two days of the Shevuot festival, he preached in the leading synagogue in Posen. One sermon deals with education, and the other is devoted to the question of non-Jewish wine. Both sermons were published the following year in Prague. In 1595, there appeared in Prague his *Netibot Olam,* a popular exposition of piety and morals. While rabbi in Posen, he was consulted in the case of an *agunah,* a woman whose husband had disappeared, there being, however, no witnesses as to his death to permit her to remarry. In the face of the timidity of other rabbis to act, Rabbi Judah found extenuating circumstances to allow her remarriage.

But Rabbi Judah's relationship with Prague was by no means severed. In 1597, when Akiba Ginzberg, Prague's popular preacher, died, Rabbi Judah was the one called to deliver the eulogy. The following year he returned to Prague, resigning his post in Posen. And now there occurred an act of partial retribution. Rabbi Jaffe resigned his position of chief rabbi of Prague and accepted a call to fill the post left vacant by Rabbi Judah's withdrawal from Posen. And at long last, Rabbi Judah became in name what he had long been in fact—the city's chief rabbi.

Rabbi Judah was now in the twilight of his life. We have little evidence of his work in the community at large. One task to which he now gave himself zealously was the publication of his remaining works. Five of his works were published between 1598 and 1600: *Tiferet Yisrael,* a philosophical study of Scriptural law, *Nezah Yisrael,* a study of the Messianic hope in Judaism, *Beer ha-Golah,* a defense of the Talmud, *Or Hadash,* a commentary on the Biblical book of Esther, and *Ner*

Mitzvah, a study of the Hanukkah festival. A number of his additional works in rabbinic law remained in manuscript and they were published posthumously. These included the *Hidushe Gur Arye*, a commentary on several tractates of the Talmud, which was published in Lemberg in 1837. A number of his manuscripts perished in a fire in 1689, an irreparable loss to Jewish culture.

Ill health and old age forced Rabbi Judah to resign his office in 1604. It had been his wish that he be succeeded by his son, Bezalel, who had in the meantime won renown as a distinguished scholar. But the old animosities asserted themselves afresh and he was refused the post. Bezalel then proceeded to Cologne where he became rabbi and head of a local academy. Rabbi Judah finally died on August 22, 1609. His wife's death followed within a year. She was buried beside him in the Prague Jewish cemetery. A common tombstone rests on their graves.[13] Thus ended the stormy career of one of the most colorful personalities in medieval Judaism.

III
Human Destiny

"All creatures were created because of the good which they embody . . . and surely the maintenance of the world and the preservation of all creatures is due to the good inherent in them. . . . And as has already been made clear, you must realize that all creatures depend on man, for they were all created for man's sake. If man does not live up to his *purpose*, then all becomes void. . . . Therefore, man must achieve the good which is his end, thereby justifying his existence, and when his existence has been justified, the whole universe has been justified, since all hinges on man. . . . Therefore a person should endeavor to cultivate good qualities. And what makes a person good so that one may say of him, 'What a fine creature he is?' One requirement is that he must be good in relation to himself. . . . The second category of good is that he be good toward the Lord who created man, to serve Him and to do His will. The third category is that he be good to others. For a person does not exist by himself. He exists in fellowship with other people. . . . And when a person acts with kindness toward others there is a bond between him and his fellowman. Thus is a person as God intended him, for he was not created that he alone should exist in the world" (Rabbi Judah, in *Derek ha-Hayim*, Warsaw 1876, pp. 8 b-9 b).

Chapter 1

THE LEGENDS ABOUT THE GOLEM

RABBI JUDAH is best known to the world as the hero of the *golem* legends. According to these stories, Rabbi Judah had labored hard to protect the Jewish community against the plots of its adversaries, but he finally became convinced that he needed more than his own strength to cope with his task. It was then that he resolved to create the *golem* (literally, any mass of matter that has remained crudely finished, without yet receiving its final form). This creature whom Rabbi Judah brought into being by invoking the miraculous potency of the secret names of God, was a giant frame of man, but a robot, without a will of his own. He was, however, the perfect tool of Rabbi Judah whose wishes he carried out implicitly.

All the *golem* stories center on feats of superhuman strength, in which some plot against the Jewish community is thwarted. In one legend, the *golem* overpowers a cart driver who was trying to smuggle the corpse of a Christian into a prominent Jew's home in order later to start a ritual murder libel against the Jews. The *golem* forces the driver to move to the town hall and to surrender with his dangerous cargo to the authorities.

In another legend the *golem* discovers the evidence that the unleavened bread for Passover had been poisoned and he helps bring the culprits to justice. One legend tells how the *golem* saves an innocent Jewish girl from apostasy. In these and in various similar legends, the *golem* has no mind of his own. He obeys mechanically what his creator ordains. It is always Rabbi Judah who directs him how to proceed.

The *golem* was always active when the amulet with the all-potent name of God was attached to him. But he became impotent when the divine name was removed from him. Rabbi Judah generally removed the amulet prior to the Sabbath to make sure that the *golem* would not desecrate the Sabbath. In one instance, Rabbi Judah forgot to remove the amulet. Almost as the Sabbath had arrived, he reminded himself. He pursued the *golem* at once and caught him in front of the synagogue just before the Sabbath service was to start. Hurriedly, he removed the amulet and the *golem* was immediately immobilized. The *golem* was finally brought to an end by Rabbi Judah when he saw the monster threaten to get out of hand. His physical remains are alleged to remain hidden to this day in the attic of the Klaus Synagogue in Prague.[1]

The belief in the creation of a *golem* was not uncommon in the Middle Ages. It is based partly on the Cabbalistic doctrine which saw in man a prototype of God on earth, who was destined to carry all existence toward perfection. The Cabbalah brings to a heightened importance the rabbinic conception of man's partnership with God in the creative development of the universe. If man is a prototype of God on earth, why should he be unable to emulate what is most characteristic of God—His role as creator?

It is based too on a doctrine of Jewish mysticism, which we shall have occasion to discuss later on, that the name of God, variously represented in the Bible, and elaborated by the secret lore of the mystics, embody the creative potency by which God formed the universe. There followed from this belief the notion that man, too, might invoke that potency to affect creation, if he only knew the right formula of letters, by which to designate the divine Name. The creation of the *golem* was but the highest use of this potency. Even as scientists today are stirred by the possibility of the synthetic creation of life, so did the alchemists and Cabbalists of the Middle Ages cherish a similar belief which they, of course, tried to achieve in their own way.

The earliest story which in its essentials resembles the creation of the *golem* is told in the Talmud. Raba is alleged to have created a man and sent him to Rab Zera who tried to converse with him, and when he received no answer, he exclaimed: "You are created by magic, return to your dust." The rationalists scoffed at these stories, but the Cabbalists, including Rabbi Loew, believed in them implicitly. Thus Rabbi Joseph Irgas whose *Shomer Emunim* is a valuable summary of Cabbalistic ideas complains at the pathetic incredulity of Maimonides, which he attributes only to the fact that he had never been enlightened by the wisdom of the Cabbalah. "It is an obvious conviction with us," he declared, "and it is made plain in many passages in the Talmud and Midrash as well, that there is a potency in 'names' and amulets to effect miraculous works. Yet Maimonides disbelieved in this!"

Solomon Ibn Gabirol was also credited with creating a *golem*. Among the better known of the medieval *golem* builders was a certain Elijah of Chelm. He was reputed to have made a *golem* out of clay and he animated it by inscribing the name of God on its forehead. The rabbi later changed his mind and tore the life-giving name from the monster's forehead, because he feared his destructive powers. Rabbi Israel Baal Shem Tob, the founder of the pietistic movement known as *hasidism*, was also alleged to have created a *golem* who acted as his personal servant.

There were parallels to the *golem* legend in the Christian community as well. Albertus Magnus is the hero in one such story. Albertus' creation, according to legend, deceived St. Thomas Aquinas who once came to vist his friend. Thinking it an emissary of the evil one, he beat it with a stick, which broke it into pieces. Paracelsus figures in a similar story. The feats of Paracelsus furnished Goethe with the material of his Faust legend. Christian mystics shared the basic doctrinal presuppositions as well as the folk-lore which flowed from them with their Jewish colleagues of the same period.[2]

Rabbi Judah's writings reveal no special pre-occupation with the magic of the practical Cabbalah, though he clearly believed in its efficacy.[3] Perhaps, the very fact that Rabbi Judah succeeded in simplifying and popularizing some of the basic doctrines of the Cabbalah, as we shall learn later on, led the people to endow him with the supernatural powers which supposedly inhered in the mastery of the Cabbalah. Folk imagination is never deterred by facts when it is launched on its work of legend building. It works with current notions, but it uses them as a totally plastic clay out of which it fashions what it pleases. All it needs is a hero whose life has made a sufficiently deep impression on the people. It is apparent that Rabbi Judah satisfied that qualification superbly well.

The *golem* legends began circulating about Rabbi Judah in the eighteenth century. They were given literary form by a group of writers, principally one Yudel Rosenberg and Chaim Bloch.[4] H. Leivick, the well-known Yiddish poet, immortalized some of these stories in his play *The Golem,* which has been produced repeatedly in this country as well as in Europe and Israel. The French and German cinema have produced films based on these stories, a rare distinction for a pious and learned rabbi.

The belief in magic, including the magic involved in the construction of the *golem,* was a blind alley in which Cabbalistic mysticism lost its course. Its essential doctrine of man and his destiny remains, nevertheless, a fruitful interpretation of life on earth. We shall trace this doctrine, in its normative characteristics, through the writings of Rabbi Judah Loew.

Chapter 2

THE DIVINE CHARACTER OF LIFE

RABBI JUDAH undertook his vast literary labors not merely in order to respond to the challenge confronting the Jewish community of his day. He was also inspired by the theologian's normal interests in dealing with the general problems of religion and life. His writings endeavor to cope with those questions which sensitive men have always raised about God and the world, about man and his destiny.

The major issue which Rabbi Judah considered in this phase of his thought was the perennial problem which has agitated scientists as well as philosophers—the quest for "a knowledge of the ultimate immutable essence that undergirds the mutable illusory world."[5] In Jewish thought this quest has assumed special urgency because of the need of meeting the intolerable contradictions between the conception of God as the Creator of the universe and the facts of general human experience. If God is the Creator and Sustainer of the universe, then all life within it ought to reflect its divine source.[6] It ought to reflect harmony, unity. Our life on earth ought to reveal qualities of wisdom and goodness, as befits the handiwork of a Creator who is all-powerful and all-good. The baffling fact, however, is that, at least in common human experience, the unity of life is obscured. It appears to be broken into a multiplicity of individual existences, of particular creatures, all differing among themselves. And instead of living with each other in harmony, these particular creatures all too often spend their substance and their energy in fierce antagonism and constant strife.

This clash between the conception of the universe as a divine creation and the facts of common experience has confronted every theology that has taken its task without evasion and without compromise. It is one of the central problems in Cabbalistic mysticism.[7] For the Cabbalist always insisted that we can know God not merely in the abstractions of thought, but also in the intimacy of direct experience, that divine elements permeate the total drama of cosmic life, as well as all individual beings who share in it. Thus it became important to deal with the world of personal experience, to find in the world about us, in man as well as in nature, the tokens of God's presence.

In resolving this paradox the Cabbalists developed the principal features of their doctrine. Existence, they taught, is at its core an unbroken unity, and all divisions within it are but an illusion; the world is essentially good, and even the evils we encounter in mundane existence somehow contribute to the advancement of life; asceticism is not the way to God, since the body is His creation and He could not have consigned it to mortification; the divine spirit which brooded over the primeval chaos to bring an ordered world into being, is still at work to extend order and harmony and to overcome the lingering irrationality and chaos in human existence; man, the crown of creation, faces the responsibility of enlisting as a co-worker with God in bringing the good to ever greater ascendency in the world, till the divine plan attain its fullest maturity and life grow to the true perfection, which is its destiny. Rabbi Judah drew on these ideas, though he often expressed them in his own idiom.

Rabbi Judah summoned men to look at the world with sensitivity and understanding, and then he was confident that they would discover its divine elements. The world we live in is the very substance out of which the Lord is busily at work to perform His design, which was first launched in that fateful hour when He willed to bring a universe into being. And His creative presence is immanent throughout all the many varied enterprises of its life. The world is a material expression of a spiritual reality. It is a kind of "garment" worn by a divine essence. "This world," Rabbi Judah declared, "enjoys a high dignity. And God's very presence, His *shekinah*, is in this world."

How can we recognize God's presence in this world? Rabbi Judah adopted a familiar theory among the Jewish mystics that the very physical attributes of the world we live in abound in suggestive parallels to the higher realm of the divine. The higher and the lower are part of one larger universe of being, and one corresponds to the other.

In the prosaic and mundane there is a veiled reference, a symbol of what is higher and more exalted. Thus Rabbi Judah took the four fundamental elements in empirical experience into which all objects in the world were generally divided in medieval science, air, wind, water, and earth, as corresponding to higher, divine elements. Air, the Hebrew *ruah*, is another name for spirit, and as such fittingly symbolizes the Torah; fire is a symbol for worship, which in Scriptural times was centered in the burning of sacrifices upon the altar; water with its beneficent effect upon the world is a symbol for deeds of loving kindness; earth which suggests stability and permanence, offers us a fitting symbol for God Himself. In these and various other parallelisms, Rabbi Judah presented the world of experience as a transparent symbol of the highest realms of divinity.

As to the alleged conflict between the multiplicity of the world's creatures, and the unity which we expect to find in God's creation, fact and intuition are both true, explained Rabbi Judah. There is an underlying unity to life, and life is also broken into a multiplicity of individual beings, each enacting its own private destiny. It all depends on the perspective from which we judge. If we judge each creature from its own standpoint, and eliminate from our consideration the divine plan in which each has its particular place, then we can only see diversity and separateness. Then we can only see a multitude of different creatures living and struggling for seemingly unrelated

FROM THE WORLD OF THE CABBALAH

ends. From the standpoint of the Creator, however, they are all integrated in a pattern of underlying harmony.

Life's fiercest antagonists are imperceptibly linked in a higher unity which makes them one. The elements of antagonism are merely different aspects of the same reality which is complex enough to embody the one as well as the other. The cleavage between those elements is, moreover, bridged by links which synthesize their differences. Thus the animal kingdom and man are linked by the monkey, which is a kind of "mediator between man and other living creatures." Middle elements exist throughout all other levels of life, and perform a like service of eliminating extremes, of mediating differences, and thus linking all existence into a unity.

The unity of life is more clearly discernible as we ascend the ladder of creation. The closer we proceed to the divine source whence all being arises, the more do we find existence fusing toward harmony, toward unity and simplicity. It is only as creation proceeds downward to realize the fullness of being with which it is impregnated, that it moves from the simple to the complex, and there sets in a process of particularization. What was whole divides into a multiplicity of fragments. Like trees which spring from one simple root and then branch out into many varying parts, so is the life of the universe. It stems from God Who is the one root of its being, and its growth is a process of expansion, of branching out, of differentiating into varying parts. All those parts persist, however, in an underlying unity. They all link to form one chain of being, one enterprise of common life.

How do we account for the existence of evil in the world? In part it derives from the fragmentary nature of our experience. When we abstract some detail from the larger context of life we may occasionally find it defective. In the larger context, however, these imperfections disappear. That detail ceases to be evil because it contributes to a larger plan, which in its over-all nature is good.

We experience evil, too, because the plan which is working

[62]

itself out in the world is still unfinished. Creation is a design working itself out in a time process, Rabbi Judah maintains. Thus it must necessarily reflect elements of imperfection. For the climax has not yet been attained. We live in a period of transition, when the world is still blundering and growing, and we suffer the pangs of growth. Rabbi Judah ascribed the enmity between nations to this immaturity among people. It results from a defect in the world, normal among creatures who have not yet developed toward an awareness of their nobler destiny.

It is striking that Rabbi Judah ascribed even Adam's disobedience of God to the same fact of immaturity. Adam had been formed in God's image, as Scripture testifies, but he was not prepared to act in accordance with that distinction. He was like a tree overhung with many branches but insufficiently rooted in the earth, which cannot endure. His growth of character was to be the process of striking his roots ever deeper into the soil of life, and thus to be established in his true dignity. As Rabbi Judah put it: "Adam was endowed with the excellence of the divine image, in which he was created. But he did not have the foundation to sustain this excellence. And this surely is a defect, to have the branches on the tree exceed what the roots can sustain. Therefore did defects attach themselves to Adam and the generations immediately following him . . . Thus their very proximity to the time of creation was responsible for their failure."

Evil arises as an incident in the movement of life toward its destiny, Rabbi Judah continued to expound, because that movement must necessarily include disintegration and death. Imperfect life forms do not voluntarily withdraw to make room for their successors in the cycle of existence. They must disintegrate and perish before they give way. That process of disintegration which is a concomitant to every cycle of growth involves pain which we, because of our limited knowledge, judge to be evil.

The constant need for the replacement of life forms by

higher achievements in the scale of creation has made it necessary, moreover, to invest what is imperfect with elements of instability. Thus Rabbi Judah explained, in the imagery of the Cabbalah, that God has released destructive forces into existence. These destructive forces constitute a realm of evil, that stands ever poised to assail life. At times, this realm of evil is characterized as an abstract force, but at times it is personalized into a host of evil spirits who are presided over by the prince of darkness and death, Sammael, the equivalent of the more familiar figure of Satan.

This realm of destructive forces is countered by a realm of positive forces that propel life ever onward on its path of self-development. The realm of positive forces corresponds to the various angelic beings whose deeds are recorded in Biblical and Talmudic writings. They are presided over by "the mighty prince, *Metatron*," a conception which the Cabbalists borrowed from the Talmud. The forces of evil have, however, only a transitory authority. As creation attains its destiny, the forces of evil will be overcome. In an epoch of transition, however, they remain a necessary element in the dialectic of growth, which is the law of the universe.

The dual character of the existent world, its apparent contradictions and its underlying harmony, Rabbi Judah pointed out, reflects the nature of the divine order which gives it being. Rabbi Judah based this conception on the Cabbalistic doctrine of the *sefirot*. The Cabbalists distinguished three principal expressions of divine activity through which God was at work to create and to sustain the universe. One realm expressed the principle of *hesed* or grace. This stands for God's absolute goodness, His unconditioned beneficence which reaches His creatures at all times, regardless of their merits, and whether they are aware of their need of it or not. It flows freely upon all beings alike, as the sunshine and the rain which warm and fructify the earth in all its fullness in an ever renewing bestowal of His bounty. Man need not seek for God's grace; the Lord confers it freely. For God is, by His very being, a bestower of beneficence upon His creation. It is precisely because this phase of divine providence is ever present that we are at times unconscious of it, but it is the sustaining power of all life.

Another realm of divine activity expresses what appears to be an opposing principle, the phenomenon of *din* or judgment. This principle is manifested in the abrupt termination of God's goodness through bringing into play visitations of punishment upon those who have violated some aspect of His law which governs the course of life in the universe. But it is more than that. It is the drawing of a fine line by which creatures are given the precise boundaries of their existence, the limitation of their resources within which to live their lives.

Between these two extremes, the Cabbalists recognized a realm of activity in which was embodied the principle of *rahamim*, or mercy. It is experienced in God's bounty which becomes available under circumstances of distress, when we are acutely aware of our need for it. Mercy differs from grace in that it is experienced only under certain conditions, while grace is free and unconditioned. This principle is a bridge that links grace and judgment, and achieves a stabilization of those elements which are essential for our world to endure.

The Cabbalists presented their doctrine in a highly technical language. The three principal expressions of divine activity were further subdivided by them into ten, the ten divine emanations, or *sefirot*. Each *sefirah* represented a distinctive level of divine energy. The ten *sefirot* they often represented by the design of a human form, in which *hesed*, grace, is the right arm, and *din*, judgment, the left arm, with *rahamim* or mercy, corresponding to the central organs. It is for this reason that what we call the negative side of life is occasionally described in the Cabbalah—it is so described by Rabbi Judah—as deriving from God's left side, while the experiences of His grace are described as deriving from His right side.

What is the relationship between the multiplicity of the *sefirot* and the one God Whom they express? As Rabbi Judah

FROM THE WORLD OF THE CABBALAH

saw it, this was but another instance where the finite mind, being unable to comprehend the truth in all its many-sidedness, is forced to portray it in fragments, speaking of multiplicity where in fact there is only oneness. There is only one God, and His providential ordering of life in the universe which seems to us divisible into three distinct categories, is in fact one coherent whole. Divisibility and fragmentation appear only from the perspective of the finite beings who receive God's providence on a kind of installment plan and who therefore see it as varied in quality. But for the illuminated mind it is all one, all serving one goal. Rabbi Judah cited the analogy of the sun and the rays of light which emanate from it. The rays appear to be many, and they appear to be something apart from the sun. Yet they are all one at their source, and they are contained in the one ball of light from which they seem to have differentiated themselves.

There is thus a rhythmic correspondence between the material world below, and the divine realm of the *sefirot*. Contradictions, particularity, differentiation—these are the appearances which reality takes on when viewed by the finite eye. But all this is illusory. The heart of all being—above as well as below—is one indivisible whole of unmarred harmony.

Rabbi Judah's conception of the universe carried special implications for man and his destiny. The divine plan which is at work in creation must also work itself out in every individual person. It is his growth that advances or retards the fulfillment of the larger plan. Thus man's life is confronted with a fateful challenge, to make the most of his own life, and thereby to carry the larger purpose of life toward fulfillment.

Rabbi Judah extolled man as the most important element in the hierarchy of life. He is the goal of all else in creation. It is he who develops the highest potentialities of nature. For nature, as launched by the Creator, has areas of incompleteness. By discovering her inherent properties and drawing upon them, man brings nature toward completion. Man outranks even the angels in value. He is a microcosm, a miniature of all the vast enterprises of cosmic life. He is, moreover, the ideal synthesis of material and divine elements, thus linking the different strata of existence into one unitary chain of being. Alone among all other creatures, he is capable of speech.

Man's highest attribute is his freedom. He is uncoerced by his own nature as to his actions, and his is the capacity to exercise sovereignty over other creatures on earth below. He walks erect in the world, and this fittingly symbolizes his higher dignity. By his nature, he was meant to be unbowed, a free being.

The Biblical designation of man as a creature formed in God's image corresponds to this attribute of his freedom, taught Rabbi Judah. "The Lord, blessed be He, is everything," he expounded, "and all things were formed for His glory. And man is similar in that he is everything among the lower creatures, all of whom were made to serve him." The angels are inferior to man because they lack this attribute of freedom. They exist ultimately for the service of man, since man is the end of creation, and they are but the emissaries of God in maintaining the enterprises of existence. Angels, moreover, are without free will. They carry out the mandates of God by the automatic workings of their natures. They do not deviate because they cannot deviate. Man, on the other hand, "who is formed in the divine image is endowed with this distinctive quality that he is autonomous as is God Who can do what He wills."

Man is distinguished objectively by his attribute of freedom. He is also distinguished subjectively, by the constitution of his being. All other beings are endowed with matter and form. Man has those also. They are his body and spirit (*nefesh*). The latter is the source of his vitalities. It makes him a living, rational being (*hai, medaber*). But in addition to his spirit, which remains enmeshed in his material self, he is also endowed with a third element, a divine soul. It is this divine soul which gives direction to his total life, and it is this soul, too, which equips man for divine pursuits and enables him to cultivate the highest reason, the divine reason embodied in the Torah.

The divine soul does not, however, function in all men equally. For the spiritual life is not pursued by man in detachment from his society, and the character of that society affects the spiritual propensities of the individual. By an act of divine determination, a unique propensity for the spiritual inheres in Israel.

Rabbi Judah pointed to a discernible sign which man bears on himself as an expression of the divine principle embodied in him—it is his facial radiance. In the Cabbalah light is seen as the most exalted phenomenon. It is a delicate and seemingly immaterial substance. It gives of itself without suffering diminution. It reveals what is hidden and permits our apprehension of whatsover has existence. And, according to Scripture, it was first in the ordered process of creation. Thus the Cabbalists looked upon light as the highest representation of reality, as the expression of God Himself. As Rabbi Judah put it; "Man's characterization as formed in the divine image derives from the fact that man was created to be king over the lower creatures even as God is King over all. . . . And this is a satisfactory explanation. But if you wish to explain the term *in His image,* the image of God, according to the truth, then explain . . . that there adhered to man's face a radiance, a divine spark, and *this* is the divine image . . . for the Lord blessed be He, is called light, for light everywhere applies to what is spiritual and immaterial."[8]

The notion that man's facial radiance embodies the divine image was a general conviction in medieval culture. It is discernible in all medieval art which represents the faces of religious figures with a halo.

Chapter 3

ON THE NATURE OF MAN

RABBI JUDAH conceded readily that man, as we find him in the world, does not always reveal his noble stature. But this derives from the fact, explained Rabbi Judah, that man's excellence is not an endowment with which he comes into the world. It is rather a development which he must attain through his own efforts. As formed by the Creator, a man is incomplete, and the whole burden of his life is a striving for completion, a quest for perfection.

Rabbi Judah saw the drive for perfection as the most important foundation of human nature. It is not by an act of casual discretion that men may decide to strive for their self-improvement. The urge to perfection has been poured into their very being, and it spurs them on to rebel against their own limitations. The most familiar expression of this urge is the phenomenon of restlessness.

Restlessness is a common human experience, but it is directed toward a specific goal. Rabbi Judah identified that goal as the craving for perfection. Only that which is complete can be at rest, "but man, being incomplete is not at rest and is therefore always striving for his completion." It was for this reason, according to Rabbi Judah, that the Bible did not characterize the creation of man as "good." After each act of creation, there follows in the Bible the statement that the Lord saw that it was good (Gen. 1). But no such characterization is given after the creation of man. The reason is "that all other creatures were perfected at the time of their creation, but man was not born complete." It is rather the capacity for growth which becomes for man the mark of that perfection which inheres in him. "And this itself," Rabbi Judah expounded, "is his perfection, that he is always striving toward the realization of potentialities and acquiring perfection."⁹

Man's necessity to strive for his own perfection rests upon two endowments of his nature, one is his free will and the other is his propensity to evil, through the promptings of the so-called "evil impulse." The former is basic to any struggle for perfection, for perfection is a condition in which an individual has learnt to choose certain courses of action in preference over alternatives. He must, however, be free to choose. If he were not free to choose, he would be without dilemmas and problems and conflicts. He would be a completed being, rather than one who must complete himself through his own development.

The human struggle for perfection rests likewise upon the fact that man is endowed with an "evil impulse." Deep within man, forces are at work which prod him on toward mischief and wrong-doing, which are ever enticing him to choose what is for his own hurt, preferring a momentary advantage over a lasting good. These forces, designated collectively as the "evil impulse," constitute the great adversary against whom man must wage his fight for the cultivation of those interests that constitute his perfection.

The "evil impulse," as the source of resistance to all our noble endeavor, has understandably been dubbed evil. Seen in larger context of life, however, even this impulse cannot really be described as evil. Indeed, were it really evil, God would not have created it as a necessary endowment of man's nature. All God's creations are intended for some beneficent end. And by the mere fact of its place in the order of creation, the "evil impulse" too must be judged as directed to some good.

What beneficent end is served by the evil impulse? This question had already been raised in the Talmud. One suggestion offered was that the so-called "evil impulse" is really the drive to self-interest, implanted in man to stimulate him toward those ends which he must pursue in his own private life, to build a house, to marry and raise a family. This impulse may lead a man to evil because, being a free agent, he may carry his desire for self-interest from the sphere of the legitimate, far beyond itself, where it becomes pernicious and objectionable.

Rabbi Judah cited this reasoning of the Talmud and he associated himself with it. But he saw the role of the evil impulse in far broader terms, as the force which makes possible the growth of character. It is as a result of the successful encounter with the evil impulse that we acquire the restraint, the discipline, which is the mark of the cultivated person. It is thus that we acquire the capacity to subject passion to the direction of reason. "More than that," he writes, after describing the view of the Talmudists, "through the help of the evil impulse, man acquires his highest excellence. . . . The evil impulse which the Lord, blessed be He, created is good because of this consideration, that when man overcomes his impulse, his excellence is above all other beings. And the Lord, blessed be He, wanted to confer merit upon man and thereby to raise him to a rank higher than that of the angels."

The struggle against the evil impulse is arduous, and we must be well prepared for it. But it is a struggle in which man can be victorious. The facts of human nature do not justify the notion that we are impotent to do good. A realization of the evil adversary against whom he must always contend should, however, make us ever vigilant and cautious in our behavior.

An indispensable help in our contest with the "evil impulse" is ever to keep before us the fact that we are only creatures, who must conform to the purposes of the Creator. When we forget our creaturely character, and assume that our own will and purpose are final, and that there is no one above us, then we must surely go astray. Thus our surrender to God for guidance at every step when we face vital decisions will give us the steering we need toward our goal.

All this must be made part of a consciously developed pattern of life. We cannot be casual and we cannot allow ourselves to improvise from step to step, from deed to deed. The

FROM THE WORLD OF THE CABBALAH

"evil impulse" was not meant to reduce us to depraved creatures, incapable of acting nobly, but the adversary is always with us to tempt, to test, and to challenge us, and we shall be unable to resist him unless we are well prepared for the encounter. But it is in that encounter that man earns his highest prize—he develops a sound moral character and becomes truly human.[10]

Chapter 4

THE UPWARD PATH

HUMAN PERFECTION for Rabbi Judah, we have seen, is a process of continuous becoming; it is not a fixed attribute, which, once achieved, gives man the final meaning of his life. Of what elements does man's perfection consist? In what direction must he develop in order to attain his true end? Rabbi Judah proposed a three-fold program. A person must endeavor to perfect his own private life; he must seek to perfect his relations with God; and he must perfect his relations with his fellow-creatures. This is the upward path by which a person moves toward the fulfillment of his highest end in life.

Our striving for perfection begins necessarily with meeting the obligations we owe to ourselves. These commence with the physical and they rise ever higher, toward the spiritual. Man is a bodily creature, in which resides a spirit, a mind. But the body is the base from which all development starts. The body must therefore be in a state of health, and its larger needs amply satisfied, if it is to serve as the faithful foundation on which to erect the full edifice of our lives. "Intelligence," said Rabbi Judah, "emerges and is born in man who is a bodily creature, for intelligence requires a material base as its carrying instrument. . . . And one does not rise to the revelation of Torah except after satisfying attributes of a material character which is its carrying instrument."

Rabbi Judah was critical of tendencies to asceticism, prevalent in many circles of his time. He had no objection to fasts or other acts of self-denial if they were intended as part of a specific effort at repentance. These may be assumed as symbols of contrition in the face of some specific sin weighing upon the soul, or, in time of disaster, to reach out more earnestly in prayer to God. There were some, however, who made asceticism a part of normal piety. They sought to reject the claims of bodily life, because in their doctrine bodily life as such was somehow evil. This Rabbi Judah denounced as error, as a distortion of the true ends of religion. "The Lord," Rabbi Judah insisted, "does not want that a person castigate himself and constantly practise fasts and be called 'a saint.' It is wicked to inflict suffering on one's body, no less than it would be to inflict it on other people."

Rabbi Judah deplored the tendency to neglect the material necessities of life, prevalent especially among scholars. This neglect is invariably avenged in their children, in whom a reaction often sets in against all scholarship and the life of the intellect. Rabbi Judah extolled the example of the great masters of the Talmud who were men of the world, even while they engaged in their scholarly endeavors. That was the great secret of their remarkable fecundity, as evidenced by the imposing literature which they left as the fruit of their intellectual labors. They achieved a proper balance between the physical and the spiritual; they did not overemphasize the spiritual at the expense of the physical. Indeed some of the most ardent recruits to a life of scholarship often came from uncultured homes, where the material life was pursued unreservedly. As "earthy" or "material" creatures they satisfy the physical prerequisites for a flowering of spiritual life.

Rabbi Judah polemicized against the pessimism of Christian doctrine, which holds the "flesh" and its claims as wholly sinful. He denounced particularly the morbid outlook on sex, which regards it as something shameful or evil, meant for man's ensnarement. It may become so if it develops into the all-absorbing interest in a person's life. In itself, however, it is one of the most glorious of life's experiences. And the comradeship of husband and wife which fuses their lives into one is surely not something "material." There is a pragmatic element in the love of husband and wife, in the sense of appreciation for incidents of mutual helpfulness. But there is another dimension to that love, transcending all pragmatic considerations. That element in love is divine; it is a spark of that fire which keeps the universe together; it is an incident of the love which is at the essence of creation itself. "All the works of the Lord are true. There is nothing shameful or degrading in any of them, and especially in man." Sex life, too, "is sanctified and holy." Similarly, there is room in life for laughter and joy and play, provided they function within a generally wholesome pattern of living.

Rabbi Judah advocated marriage as a fundamental moral obligation of a person. And it is significant that he held the goal of marriage to go beyond procreation. It achieves its highest significance in the love and companionship between husband and wife. The male and female principles are indispensable to each other in human life even as they are in the universe at large. A wife is the completion of a man's personality. The dissolution of marriage through divorce is a kind of murder. For it is the undoing of a person. A complete person is a man and a woman fused in the harmonious relationship of married life.

Rabbi Judah's tribute to the spiritual significance of sex followed a general trend in Cabbalistic mysticism. Rabbi Moses ben Nahman, one of the early Cabbalists, for instance, had written in a similar vein. Criticizing Maimonides whose writings reveal the Aristotelian disdain of sex life, he declared in his famous *Igeret ha-Kodesh* (A Letter on Holiness): "It is not true, as our rabbi and master assumed in his *Guide to the Perplexed,* praising Aristotle for teaching that the sexual urge is a source of shame to us. God forbid that the truth should be in accordance with the teachings of the Greek. . . . The act of sexual union is holy and pure. . . . The Lord created all things in accordance with His wisdom and whatever He created cannot possibly be shameful or ugly. . . . When this union is for the sake of Heaven nothing can be nobler or cleaner. . . . When a man is in union with his wife in a spirit of holiness and purity, the Divine Presence is with them." The Cabbalists saw the very dynamism of existence as the yearning of masculine and feminine principles to find each other, and by their juncture, to beget new life. They even differentiated the ten *Sefirot,* which emanate from the ineffable oneness of God to beget the finite universe, as male and female. What was true of the universe, the macrocosm, could not be false in man, the microcosm. The act of sexual union was therefore seen as an instance of the universal rhythm of all existence.

Rabbi Judah was also within the basic presuppositions of the Cabbalah in the respective roles which he assigned to husband and wife within the family. The Cabbalists who read the distinction between male and female principles into the structure of the most fundamental forces in the universe, identified these principles as active and passive, respectively. The male principle, which is active, they ranked higher than the passive female principle. Since passivity was generally looked upon as an attribute of matter, while it is the spiritual which imposes form on matter, they also spoke of the female and male principles as matter and form. In the light of these ideas Rabbi Judah looked upon the husband as the leader in all spiritual affairs, while the wife's initiative was to be respected in the management of the home and in all worldly affairs.

Rabbi Judah spoke of the importance of planning for one's economic security. One should not strive for riches. These are a form of bondage; a person becomes involved in and tied down to his possessions, and to that extent he is robbed of his independence. However, one should endeavor to become self-sustaining by engaging in a useful occupation or business. It is important to provide comfortably for one's family, for most family quarrels are rooted in difficulties which arise when the family is in want.

The clue to a valid pattern of life consists in the realization that man is not wholly spiritual and not wholly material. His nature is a fusion of both elements, and the good life must satisfy both. The physical life is a preliminary to higher levels of life. "It is proper for man to reject the affairs of this world, namely the affairs that are without substance. However, the desirable works of this world are desirable before God, even though they are physical in character. . . ." There can be no leaps in our rise to our destiny. The peak to which we aspire is beyond the world but we must climb to it step by step. And the ladder on which we rise has its foot in the pursuit of those interests by which we satisfy the claims of our own bodily natures.[11]

The relationship between man and God, Rabbi Judah explained, derives from the fact that God is the Creator and man, His creation. There is a natural drive in all organisms toward whatever completes them. Man, left to himself, is incomplete, inadequate, and he feels drawn toward God "Who is the source of his sustenance, and without Whom he cannot have being."

The drive in man leading him to God is the emotion of love, as "all things love whatever is their completion, and God is the completion of man." The love of God, in its highest expression, is a disinterested love. It is not a means to any other end. It does not expect rewards, and it is not even a return for favors previously granted. It is rooted in man's natural drive for self-completion. When man knows his true dependence on God, he becomes aware of his insufficiency, and he is overcome by a great yearning for God Who alone can make him whole. This love of God, like true friendship, will persist regardless of what befalls us, in joy and in sorrow alike.

The relationship between man and God also exists on the level of fear, or awe. This is engendered by contemplating the majesty and grandeur of God. Fear as such is negative, and is a depressing rather than a joyous experience. At best it can inspire people to avoid evil. Only love can inspire the positive quest for the good. And the fear of God must therefore rank lower than the love of God.

The fear of God, Rabbi Judah expounded, exists, however, on another level, too; and those who attain it have attained

[77]

the highest type of relationship with God. On this level the fear of God is a continuous self-effacement before Him. It is man's highest response to the fact that he is the creation and God is the Creator, upon Whom he continues to lean throughout his life. This is accompanied by a dread of doing anything displeasing to Him, anything that might break the bond with Him. Fear in this sense is really a derivative of love. "For he who loves one concentrates on heeding his wishes in all things possible, that there be no estrangement in this love, and therefore he fears to transgress his will even in small matters. . . ." The fear of God is the highest fruit of all the development, of all the learning, human and divine, which man attains in the world.

This type of fear even outranks the love of God, for it is distinctively the relationship which man, at his best, can enter with God. Love is possible between equals, and it may, therefore, prevail among creatures. But fear does not apply to a relationship among creatures. For all creatures are equal, and there is no justification for one to efface himself before another. This type of fear is uniquely appropriate between the creatures and the Creator, and is therefore the noblest attitude of man toward God.

The love and the fear of God, obviously, do not exclude each other. They are supplementary emotions, each of which has its proper scope within the complexity of human experience. "The true service of God is through love and fear. . . . For in their ultimate character, love and fear flow from the same source. . . . And it is not proper that there be fear without love or love without fear. There are, however, situations which call for love alone, and there are situations which call for fear alone. But within man himself love and fear should exist simultaneously."[12]

Our effort at self-development, Rabbi Judah added, must, finally, include a perfection of our relations with our fellow creatures. Our solicitousness for the fellow creatures who share the world with us derives on one level from the love and the fear of God. The man who sees only the world of living creatures, with himself as the final authority for disposing of them, may be tempted to play the unlimited sovereign, and to "seek dominion over all." When, however, he acknowledges God as sovereign, he necessarily learns that others have equal status with him. The very fact that God saw fit to give them existence, confers upon them value. "The love of people is at the same time a love for God. For when we love some one, we necessarily love his handiwork. . . . And therefore one who loves God cannot but love His creatures, while if he should hate the creatures he cannot love the God who formed them. And thus the dignity of one's neighbor, who was created in the divine image, is equivalent to God's dignity."

Our solicitousness for other creatures is also reinforced by considering man's place in the universe. If the universe comprises a unity, with each individual representing a unique element in the design of the total whole, then life is inter-dependent, and individuals complement one another. Thus we must concern ourselves with the welfare of others because individually we are not self-sufficient, because we depend for the enlargement of our lives upon linking them with the lives of others.

Man's glorious distinction of being fashioned in the image of God is not an attribute which is possessed by single individuals. Human beings are all uniquely different. It is only through the integration of all the unique human elements, represented by all human individuals, that we move toward the wholeness of the human pattern. And it is only as that pattern reaches wholeness that it may be said to reflect the divine image.

The welfare of other creatures, as Rabbi Judah saw it, is really then our own welfare, too. For we share a common destiny, and we are part of every other being who inhabits the earth with us. Like the fate of any one organ which affects the life of the rest of the body, so does the fate of any individual affect the lives of all others who comprise the larger body of the human community. Their lives are pledged to our welfare, as our life is pledged to theirs. Our love for one another is in a certain sense a love for what is really part of ourselves; and one who hates others is really guilty of self-hatred.

The empirical facts of social life frequently reveal individuals and nations as enemies, in conflict with one another. But, Rabbi Judah expounded, there is no real conflict as far as their true interests are concerned. For parallelling their unique natures, God provided unique areas in life for each of them. Like the individual hair on the human head, each individual person has his own place in the world from which to draw his strength and the vitalizing energy of his life.

We become enemies instead of friends, Rabbi Judah continued, when we go beyond the scope of our own legitimate sphere and seek what is not really ours. To some extent our very differentiation, our unique natures and perspectives, begets a propensity for quarrelsomeness. For each tends to be impressed only with his own excellence, and to be unmindful of his neighbor's. It is only in the divine plan that there is a distinctive sphere for each, and "thus is there a basis for peace between them so that one does not enter the sphere of the other, and each one remains autonomous." But most people do not see each other from the perspective of the divine plan, and this failure is the mark of our immaturity and imperfection.

The growing perfection in our relations with others includes the recognition of our true place in the world, and a consequent respect for the boundaries of our own, and of others' lives. As we achieve this recognition, we can heed increasingly the imperatives of our natures which call for our being friends instead of enemies. In increasing measure we must thus strive to harmonize human differences and to establish peace in the home, among friends, and peace in society at large.[13]

Rabbi Judah regarded the Torah's prohibition of marriages among close blood relations as a means of bringing greater unity into the world. Had such marriages been permitted, there would have developed ever more closely knit family groups, without crossing from one to the other The fact that men must go outside their family circle to marry, tends to create new unities among diverse groups of people.

God has further provided for a greater unity among human beings by not permitting the acquired excellences of learning and character to be transmitted as an inheritance from generation to generation. If that had been the case, society would have been dichotomized into permanently distinct castes, and the underlying unity among men would have been obscured. The equality of all human beings is effectively maintained by the constant crossing of boundaries, with mediocrities frequently descending from distinguished families, and great people emerging from humble backgrounds.

The clash of ideas, which so often divides people into hostile camps, is likewise based on a perversion of facts. Rabbi Judah was primarily concerned with accounting for the multiplicity of controversies among the Talmudists, in their interpretations of the Torah, but his exposition has general interest. Because we are unique personalities we each see a unique aspect of the truth. The total truth is beyond any of us. Only God has the whole, the absolute truth, because He alone has absolute existence. But each person in his own unique way comes upon some portion of truth. In each body of ideas there is a core of vital truth which complements the core of truth in another system of ideas that seems to be its rival. "As the multiplicity of creatures derives from God, so does the multiplicity of ideas, in their essence, derive from Him, blessed be He; and although the ideas appear to negate one another they nevertheless each have a sphere of legitimate meaning...."

The admixture of falsehood and exaggeration which comprises the truth of any body of ideas is responsible for the apparent clash. In certain systems of ideas there will be more falsification, while in others there will be a closer approximation to the truth. But each of them has some truth. There is some truth even in idolatry. It is a partial recognition of the divine power in the universe. Its sin is its partiality, its lifting of an aspect of God's power, or a manifestation of it, for supreme reverences as though it were God. But it represents a glimmer of the truth that there is a power transcending life who is the source of all its blessings.

There are occasions when we have to act, in decisions of law, for instance, and then we may have to reject certain opinions in favor of others. In such instances Rabbi Judah demanded a ready bending on the part of the individual in favor of the majority view. "It may be that they knew better." And there are occasions, too, when certain ideas must be combatted because they function as a destructive force in the world. Rabbi Judah himself fought vigorously against Azariah dei Rossi's *Meor Enayaim*, a work of historical criticism on the sources of Jewish tradition, which he regarded as a pernicious attack against the validity of fundamental teachings in Judaism. "Contentiousness is a very offensive quality, but it is not offensive at all times. Thus contention with wicked men is good."

It is, however, for us to know, Rabbi Judah argued, that when we reject one idea in favor of another, we are choosing between a lesser and a greater truth, and not between a complete falsehood and a complete truth. Men follow falsehood because of some fragments of truth which are mingled with it. Total falsehood could not gain any credence at all in the world. As Rabbi Judah put it; "And what we reject must not be rejected as though it had no substance of truth at all, just as we dare not reject any of the works of the Lord, although among them there are some which are more perfect and truer."

The clash of ideas is, like the tensions among people generally, a preliminary to the process of integration. For the clash of ideas is the act of vital clarification. This accounts for the abundance of controversy among the rabbis of the Talmud. Each such controversy is an effort at clarity, which is to be achieved not by ignoring any aspect of truth, but by reckoning with all perspectives and all diverse ideas on every subject under discussion. As Rabbi Judah put it: "Each one receives a particular aspect of the truth, in accordance with his mental portion. . . . And when these are all gathered up, we have the truth in all its manysidedness."

The truth can only emerge purer and clearer from each controversy. Defending religious liberty and the free criticism of prevailing religious dogmas against the dominant church policy of his day, which attempted to suppress all dissident ideas, Rabbi Judah on one occasion declared: "It is improper to suppress the views of an opponent, but it is more fitting to encourage them and to ponder their meaning. Thus will a person attain a fuller faith. It would therefore be wrong to silence a person who expresses himself against religion, with the injunction: 'Do not speak thus.' "[14]

Rabbi Judah's defense of religious dissent was not formulated as a general doctrine of freedom. It was directed at those who sought the suppression of Judaism. But men often come upon general principles as a result of sensing their cogency in the struggle with personal problems. Rabbi Judah's defense of the right to dissent is, moreover, a direct implication of his general conception of the uniqueness of the individual. It remains a significant pronouncement, foreshadowing the ideas of John Stuart Mill in his celebrated essay on Liberty, and is part of the ideological foundation for a democratic society.

Chapter 5

THE FOUNDATIONS OF WORLD ORDER

RABBI JUDAH'S doctrine of man led directly to an analysis of society, and to an examination of the forces that disrupt the harmony which should prevail in it. True harmony among men, Rabbi Judah taught, depends on the delineation of the precise boundaries encompassing the particular individuals and nations. The quest for world harmony is then a quest for justice. For justice is a state of human balance where each individual person or community is in full possession of its unique sphere, within which to enact its destiny. Every unique life has been provided for by the Creator with a unique place in the world, and as long as men stay within the frontiers of their own proper places, the world will be in harmonious equilibrium.

The grossest violation of the principle of harmony is the oppression of man by man and nation by nation. Man by nature was meant to be independent and self-determining; it is not proper, Rabbi Judah declared, "that he should be subservient to another."

We have already noted Rabbi Judah's protests against the oppressive rule exercised by the upper classes in his own community. His concern with justice is further reflected in his discussions of the prerogatives of the king.

The king, according to Rabbi Judah, enjoys no intrinsic superiority over other men. His sovereignty is not inherent to his person, "since it is possible for some one else to be king, inasmuch as all men are by their inherent nature eligible to be king." The king's office exists to perform a specific function in the state: "The business of the king is not that he be for himself, but that he attend to the needs of the people . . . and improve their affairs in whatever respects they are defective. In discharging these duties, moreover, he must concentrate on the needs of the poor, the lowly in spirit, rather than upon those of men in high station."

The king is really the servant of the people, not their master. Being "subservient to the people, pledged to them," a king may elicit love from his subjects, but not fear. Fear in the sense of self-effacement before a superior, is applicable only toward God. For God alone is man's superior. Intrinsically the king is no superior to even the humblest citizen.

The religious affirmation of a universal loyalty to God has frequently been resented by earthly sovereigns as an infringement on their own power. As Rabbi Judah explained it: "Obedience to a religion which carries the authority of a heavenly King withdraws man from the authority of a king who is flesh and blood." This has often led to conflict between religion and the representatives of the state, the latter being anxious "to display an exalted authority and have people heed the commands of the mortal king and to do away with the commands of the King of the universe." Rabbi Judah maintained that the persecutions of Jews at various times was inspired, at least in some measure, by this tendency of the state to seek absolute loyalty and power over the lives of people. It was states such as these, which seek to place themselves above the loyalties men owe to God, Rabbi Judah explained, that the Jewish liturgy referred to as *malkut zadon,* a wicked state, for whose downfall it implored divine intercession.

The state is a human institution, arising to meet conventional human needs; it is not rooted in the inherent pressures of nature or in the will of God. During a period of human immaturity, when men are incapable of living in true freedom, the state may be a social necessity. However, when the human being has attained true maturity, the state will become obsolete. It will finally be done away with as an unnatural infringement upon human liberty, and a perversion of life's inherent simplicities.

Rabbi Judah was similarly emphatic in his denunciation of national oppression. Nations are not an artificial but a natural differentiation in humanity. "Each nation is endowed with a distinctive essence . . . with a character pattern of its own." Each nation occupies a distinctive chamber in the mansion of universal existence and it is called on to play a unique role in the world. National distinctiveness is maintained through unique culture patterns, including religion, language, diet, and especially through the possession of a distinctive national territory.

Any suppression of these vital elements by which a nation maintains itself is an injustice, and disturbs the harmonious equilibrium of the human community. "According to the order of existence it is not proper that one nation should be subservient to another. . . . For the Lord created each nation to be unto itself. . . . The oppression of nation by nation does not conform to the proper order of existence, for it is proper that each nation shall be free."

The extension of freedom for individuals and for nations is a vital step forward in the realization of God's plan in history. This extension of freedom is bound to come in ever increasing measure, despite temporary setbacks, since it rests not on the casual interests of people at a certain time, but on the fundamental imperative of all existence. Behind it is the pressure of man's very destiny, as ordained by the God who fashioned him.

The oppression of any one people is a threat to all others. For it betrays a general loss of respect for human life, and what is to impede the extension of the tyrant's design to other human groups? This thought is suggested in Rabbi Judah's comment on *Esther* 3:15. After the decree was published projecting the extermination of the Jews in Persia, the Bible reports: "The city of Shushan was perplexed." "Behold," observed Rabbi Judah, "the preponderant population in Shushan were of the nations, not Jews, but they could not account for these designs against an entire people. ... They were perplexed about this and said, 'Today Haman consigned this people to slaughter, and tomorrow Haman will consign another people.'"

The ideal basis for human organization is justice, but a precise justice, Rabbi Judah warned, cannot be attained by man. Only God can know the exact frontiers of the life of each individual or nation, where the proper place begins for one, and ends for another. For man to hew to an uncompromising line with everyone seeking all that properly belongs to him, in a spirit of rigorous justice, would only embroil the world in endless claims and counter-claims; and the result of such an attitude would be recurring explosions of individual and group violence. The unwillingness ever to yield on "rights" will, moreover, eventually lead a person to invade the rights of others. Such a person will tend to take with violence, if necessary, whatever he cares to claim as his own. One who becomes accustomed to be unyielding for his own, will in the end be in possession of ill-gotten gains.

It is important that men recognize that there is a proper place for each individual and for each nation; and that each has rights which the others dare not infringe upon. A satisfactory order of human relations cannot, however, be built on the strict pursuit of justice. It can be built on the pursuit of charity and loving-kindness, on the readiness to overlook "rights" in a spirit of mutual service and mutual love. In the human body each organ thrives by drawing upon the contributions of the other organs; one is pledged to the other in common service. "And similarly in society as a whole one is pledged to help the other." The most significant human attribute to cultivate "is loving-kindness . . . not justice or any other attribute."[15]

The implementation of the ideal of loving-kindness calls for respecting the dignity of every human being. A person enjoys that dignity by virtue of his being a creature of God and a person, not by virtue of any special status he may have acquired in the world. The non-Jew, the pagan, is to be accorded that dignity, for he, too, is a creature of God, made in the divine image.

To respect the dignity of a person means to avoid doing anything that will embarrass or hurt him or that will injure his reputation in the world. The small talk which undermines the standing of other people, which slanders their character or ridicules their failings, is one of the gross sins against which Rabbi Judah inveighed constantly. A person's speech reflects his character, even as the fruit reflects the quality of the tree upon which it grows.

We are to respect the dignity of even a wicked man, Rabbi Judah insisted. Submerged beneath his wickedness is a divine element, for every power exercised by a person is a divine endowment, even though that power may be used for evil ends. Occasionally, the skills and talents which are misused by evil men are recovered for posterity in a subsequent generation. Children arise in whom that power lives on, and who purify it and dedicate it to good ends.

The destruction of a wicked man is from God's point of view a tragedy, a grievous dissipation of the assets of the universe. It should occasion no rejoicing in us either, Rabbi Judah maintained, unless that downfall was accompanied by a full realization of the sins that produced it and a consequent attempt to repent. "If the downfall did not serve to eliminate the practice of wickedness, it is certainly not good, even though it befell a wicked person, and it should occasion no rejoicing; such rejoicing is fully prohibited."

The needy among us are entitled to assistance, to the full measure of their need. But even recipients of charity are entitled to be treated in accordance with their dignity as persons. One must not expect them to be unduly subservient to those according them aid. They have a right to that aid. Material aid, however, is not enough. There are times when it is even more important to comfort a person in need. Words spoken in friendship may accomplish more than a gift of money. Private feuds do not affect the claim of the needy for assistance. One must be charitable even toward an enemy; it is a good way of converting him to a friend. Where a person refuses to give charity, it is legitimate to coerce him, "for charity is an obligation;" it does not rest on a private magnanimity or "the prompting of the heart." Callousness toward human beings is the essential mark of a wicked man.

Man's relation to his fellow-creature does not confine itself to the human level. It is as universal as God's creation itself. Man must treat with compassion every living being. For God is the father of all creatures. They are all part of the pattern of life. And they are all entitled to considerate treatment at the hands of man.

Existence is differentiated into varying levels of values, but, Rabbi Judah expounded, there is some value in all that exists, and man's relationship to any creature must reflect a consciousness of its dignity and worth. "The whole universe belongs unto the Lord as He created all, and whatever belongs unto the Lord is sacred. And do not say 'although all are His creatures, they do not all serve Him as do certain specific creatures that act in His service, and therefore only the latter are sacred.' . . . For this is not so. All have been created to serve the Lord: all have been created for His glory. All are part of the ensemble of creation and it is His creatures that manifest the glory of his work. Therefore everything is sacred unto the Holy Name, blessed be He."[16]

Chapter 6

ON VINDICATING CREATION

THE UPWARD PATH by which man must travel in his quest for perfection is a fateful adventure. What is at stake is not only man's own life. It is the pattern of all existence, the permeating purpose of the universe.

Man's appearance on the arena of existence and the destiny he was to enact therein constituted, according to Rabbi Judah, the goal of all creation. Rabbi Judah rejected the doctrine of Maimonides that the purpose of the universe remains shrouded in the mysterious will of God. It is possible for man to decipher that mystery, Rabbi Judah maintained.

God had brought creation into being, according to Rabbi Judah, because there is greater perfection in actualizing the potential than allowing it to remain frozen in its non-realized state. God in Whom is embodied all perfection would not allow the universe to remain a dormant possibility of His power. A creator in action is more perfect than a creator in potentiality. And thus instead of permitting the universe to remain an idea asleep in the divine mind, He clothed it with the materiality of creation.

There is a clear purpose for every creature also, in the sense of a goal to which it must direct its life, taught Rabbi Judah. That purpose is to glorify its Creator. It is not that God is in need of His creatures' glorification. Each creature, however, need its own vindication, and it achieves it to the extent that it acknowledges God's sovereignty and conforms to His will. "It is true that God is not dependent on being glorified by His creatures. . . . But all creatures justify their creation by the fact that they honor the Lord blessed be He."

FROM THE WORLD OF THE CABBALAH

Every creature has its purpose, its function to fulfill in God's plan, and it glorifies God by being true to its purpose, by being what God wanted it to be. The multitude of creatures who inhabit the world cannot however attain their vindication without man. For the entire enterprise exists for his sake and he is the crucial link who brings the entire chain of being into a unity. When man fails to travel the upward path, when he withdraws from the fulfillment of his destiny, then catastrophe has set in throughout the cosmos. The purpose of all existence has been frustrated. The chain of being which forges all existence into a unity has been severed. Creation has reversed itself, retreating back again from order to chaos. It is man's supreme obligation not to permit this. His life must contribute toward the world's greater perfection, not its disintegration.

Each creature glorifies God in its own unique way, since the life and destiny of each is differentiated from every other in some unique fashion. This applies to persons as well. Human perfection is general and, in its general norms, is the same for all men. It includes our obligations to ourselves, our duties to our Creator, and a responsibility for the welfare of our fellow creatures. Because our destinies are, however, differentiated and unique, our perfection must also express itself distinctively, from each according to his position in life.

The king and princes glorify God if they acknowledge a sovereignty higher than the sovereignty of their own state, if they respect the sovereignty of God, and rule "without robbing and oppressing people as is the custom among princes." The judges glorify God "if they are God-fearing in judgment." The elders add their hymn of glory to God, if they teach the people, while younger men offer theirs if they steer clear of sin and are able to keep their passions under control. Those who live in larger cities manifest a special piety if they can overcome the vices of urban life, the love of pleasure and of luxury.

We glorify God not with formal exercises of conscious adoration, but with our total existence. A person who directs his

[91]

life toward the love of God, raises every activity he engages in to the level of divine service, even eating and drinking. For life is all one enterprise and its ultimate end determines the quality of life as a whole.

    A person thus stands not only as a highly privileged member in the hierarchy of life. He also stands under a high commitment. In some special way every person completes the universe. If he does not play his part, he injures the pattern of all existence, and defeats God's purpose in having created a world. By playing his part, he helps fulfill the highest purpose underlying the whole vast drama of God's creation.[17]

IV
Reason and Faith

"The Mishnah has criticized the reprehensible person who puts all his thoughts and aims upon this physical world. But Rabbi Eleazer (in Mishnah, Abot, ch.3) criticized men who represent the opposite. They believe they must turn to reason exclusively and they deprecate everything which has any aspect of the physical. They desecrate the altar offerings in the Temple because they say God does not eat or drink and, therefore, there is no sense offering such things as sacrifices to Him. . . . They despise the festivals because they say the holidays offer physical pleasure for man, in eating and drinking, and they claim that one does not achieve divine ends in this manner. They dissolve the covenant of Abraham (the rite of circumcision) and say it is despicable to think that God would make a covenant with this organ which is a source of shame and dishonor. . . . And they likewise disparage their fellowman by saying that man is a material creature and he is not of much worth. They also read improper interpretations into the Torah, treating irreverently the commandments which apply to bodily life, all because they pursue the intellectual and renounce the physical. These men for whom the physical world is of no value and physical deeds, even when they are good deeds are of no significance, who say that man's only interest should be the quest for enlightenment . . . will have no share in the world to come." (Rabbi Judah, in *Derek ha-Hayim*, p.48b)

CHAPTER 1

THE CHALLENGE OF RATIONALISM

IN 1572 AZARIAH BEN MOSES DEI ROSSI completed his epoch-making work *Light unto the Eyes*, which was soon offered to the world in Hebrew under the title *Meor Enayim*. Azariah had lived in Mantua, Italy, where he practiced medicine. In his spare time he studied Hebrew antiquities and wrote poetry. The earthquake in Ferrara in 1570 which took a toll of more than 200 lives reminded him of the transitoriness of existence, and it engendered in him the yearning to create a work that would serve as a kind of monument to his name. He was goaded to undertake his labors, too, by a casual question from a Christian scholar who had inquired whether the Jews had preserved the Hebrew text of the well-known work of the Apocrypha, the *Letter of Aristeas*. Azariah was struck by the fact that not only this work but the entire body of Hellenistic Jewish literature was little known among his people. At once he was aware of his mission, and he undertook to fill this gap.

The *Meor Enayim* consists of three parts. The first is an account of the Ferrara earthquake; the second is a translation of the *Letter of Aristeas;* the third is a study in Jewish history and archeology. Azariah was the first to acquaint the Hebrew reader with the works of Philo and with the Greek translation of the Bible, the *Septuagint*.

Azariah's work filled a serious gap in Jewish knowledge, but what startled his readers was the critical tone with which he allowed himself to speak of Jewish tradition. He challenged the accuracy of the commonly accepted chronology of the Jewish past. Most serious of all was the fact that he scoffed at many passages in the Talmud. He exposed the ignorance of the Talmudists in astronomy. He endeavored to show that the Talmudists frequently indulged in exaggerations and that their pronouncements, especially on historical subjects, are unauthentic and cannot be taken seriously.

There was, for instance, the story about the end of Titus, the Roman general responsible for burning the Temple. According to the Talmudic version (Gittin 56b), a tiny fly entered his brain and for seven years bored and bored until he died. One of the Talmudists adds to this that its mouth was of copper and its nails of iron. For Azariah this was nothing but a fanciful tale, the figment of an undisciplined rabbinic imagination.

Azariah also questioned the exaggerated importance attached by the Talmudists to various religious regulations. He cited the opinion in the Talmud that Jerusalem was destroyed because her people were brazen and lost a sense of distinction between the great and the small among them. Similarly he cited the statement that a person who embarrassed his neighbor had forfeited his share in the world to come. His general conclusion was that the *agadah,* the entire non-legal portion of the Talmud, must not be taken seriously, that its authors developed this material only for the sake of the common people, to appeal to their imagination and to create incentives for their obedience to the law of the Torah.

In Cabbalistic circles especially there was a violent reaction against the *Meor Enayim.* Dei Rossi did not attack the Cabbalah as such. But his approach to tradition was the very antithesis to the one pursued by the Cabbalists. The very stories of the Talmud which Dei Rossi disparaged were the poetic symbols and allegories through which they conveyed mystical philosophy. The Cabbalah invested all the traditional expressions of religion with a new vitality and significance, and they raised religious loyalties to a new depth of feeling. Cabbalists were therefore most sensitive to every attack launched by rationalists against traditional Judaism.

Moses Provinçali, who combined with his interest in Cabbalah a many-sided education in general knowledge, and a friend of Azariah, was the first to denounce his work. The leading rabbis of Italy, where the Cabbalah had a wide following, joined in the chorus of denunciation. Joseph Caro, then a leading figure among the Cabbalists in Safed, Palestine, planned an edict of excommunication against the work, but he died before his plan could be carried out. In Azariah's own home city of Mantua an edict was promulgated prohibiting the *Meor Enayim* to any one who had not yet attained twenty-five years of age—except by special permission from the religious authorities.

Soon after the publication of the *Meor Enayim* a copy was shown to Rabbi Judah Loew. A lover of learning whose interests were many-sided, Rabbi Judah hailed the work, and rejoiced in it, "as the groom rejoices in meeting his bride." But as he continued reading it, his delight changed into consternation. "Woe unto the eyes that behold such things and unto the ears that hear them," he exclaimed. "Cursed be the day on which these matters were made public. How could this person speak against the sages, when he does not understand their simplest statements, surely not their more subtle and deeper teachings? Yet he speaks against them as though they were his own contemporaries! Such brazenness has not happened in Israel until this generation. . . . This is one of the heretical books which one is forbidden to read. . . ." This denunciation of Azariah dei Rossi's *Meor Enayim* was only one shot which Rabbi Judah fired in his campaign against rationalism.

The conflict between religion and rationalism was a major theme in the writings of Rabbi Judah. Jewish culture in the 16th century was dominated by rabbinic learning, above all by the Talmud and its copious commentaries. But every age has had its bold spirits who manage to cross the frontiers of conventional life, to explore new paths. And the time of Rabbi Judah had its circle of these bold spirits, men who dabbled in philosophy and science and who tried to relate their new truth to the precepts of their traditional faith.

FROM THE WORLD OF THE CABBALAH

The source of this rationalism was ultimately the writings of the Greek philosophers, especially Aristotle, whose ideas remained the foundation of every medieval conception of the universe, but it was not really necessary to go to the Greek originals for these views. They were amply represented by Jewish writers. There were men like Saadia and Ibn Daud and, above all, as we have noted before, Maimonides, whose writings formed a kind of apocryphal wisdom in Jewish tradition, which exerted a haunting fascination upon these braver spirits in the Jewish community. Maimonides had subjected Greek thought to critical evaluation, and on all crucial issues he vindicated his religious tradition. Yet, in spots, the line he drew came dangerously close to the edge of the road. There were others like Gersonides and Albalag who allowed even greater sway to the ideas of Aristotle.

The spokesmen of rationalism varied in their doctrine, but essentially they were all under the spell of the Greek exaltation of reason. Reason alone, they taught, brings man to the highest vistas of truth and to the noblest attainments of the good life. These men did not declare themselves as atheists; they did not break formally with religion. But they reformulated the basic doctrines of religion, to make them conform to a rational outlook on the universe. They believed in God, but they thought of God as absolute Reason, as Mind, and His actions in the processes of life they brought within the workings of natural causality. They refused to accept the possibility of miracles as arbitrary violations of natural law. They denied man's centrality in the hierarchy of life. Before the heavenly bodies above, man appears lowly and insignificant, and he must be judged distinctly below them in value.

The way to God, which is indeed man's highest good, these men held obtainable only through the intellectual life, through the acquisition of knowledge, especially of the highest strata of nature, of the spheres and the stars which, according to Aristotle were living beings possessed of souls, or as he called them, "Intelligences." The method of philosophy is our only sure road to truth, and it is the one and only door by which we may move ever closer to God.

Rationalism, no matter what its source, revealed its greatest peril to the religious life in its disparagement of the sacred Scriptures. In the Bible and especially the Talmud the rationalists found a very naive conception of God. These works abounded in parables and legends which seemed absurd to sophisticated minds. These works, too, center religion on physical acts, on conformity to law, especially ritual, which from the perspective of rationalism could not possibly represent man's highest good. The conclusion to which rationalists tended was that the sacred Scriptures and the way to life which they embodied were addressed only to the uneducated multitudes, who could not be expected to rise to intellectual pursuits in which alone was a mature religion to be found. The Torah was thus reduced more or less to a man made work through which the leaders of organized religion endeavored to keep the masses of humanity to a prescribed discipline.

Maimonides saved the Biblical text from such disparagement by assuming that it spoke in other than what seemed to be its literal meaning. He proposed a system of figurative interpretations of the Bible, which made it into a vehicle of a higher truth. But what was this higher truth, according to him, which the Bible conveyed? It was the theories of Aristotle, his physics and metaphysics. In the days when Aristotle was assumed to speak the last word on all matters of worldly knowledge, this was perhaps a great gain. But in the 16th century Aristotle had long since been deposed from his lofty pedestal, and what Maimonides had done appeared to be a great affront to the Bible.

As for the Talmud, Maimonides had allowed himself even greater liberties. He had ruled the entire non-legal material of the Talmud, the *agadah,* as without binding authority, and he did not hesitate to reject beliefs freely entertained by the Talmudists, simply because they did not jibe with his rationalist pre-suppositions. This critical approach to the Talmud seemed especially offensive in the sixteenth century because it played directly into the hands of Christian polemicists who had made the Talmud a special target in their attacks against Judaism.

We have noted that religion was also challenged by the impact of the new science which had made its appearance in the sixteenth century. The new science was built on other foundations than those on which Maimonides had built his religious synthesis. The Maimonidean synthesis was built on the philosophy of Aristotle which sought truth by way of speculation, through the operations of syllogistic reasoning. The new science was built on direct contact with reality, on the observation of nature, on actual experience with the facts of life. Indeed the scientific movement which began to emerge in the sixteenth century was in many respects a revolt against Aristotle, many of whose teachings were now proven fallacious. Yet some of the philosophic generalizations deriving from Aristotle were carried over into the new age. And while science is not based on the Aristotelian syllogism, it proved no friendlier to a religion which took its truth from a revealed Scripture.

At a time of fierce persecutions, when Jews were under continued pressure to betray their faith and find release through apostasy, the challenge boldly offered in the name of reason and of science was especially ominous. It threatened the Jewish community from within. For it had become all too clear that in the hour of testing those who had been touched by sophistication were weakest in their faith, while the people of simple piety generally exhibited the greatest steadfastness.[1]

Chapter 2

REASON HAS HER LIMITS

RABBI JUDAH'S DEFENSE of religion had little in common with the obscurantism which prevailed in some circles and which had sought to ban all pre-occupations with science and philosophy. As an exploration of the physical universe, the sciences offer a most valuable body of knowledge, and it is certainly proper to cultivate them.

The natural order is God's creation, Rabbi Judah explained, and how could one oppose the investigation into any phase of God's handiwork? Indeed, a knowledge of the vastness and the grandeur of creation leads to a deeper love for God, to a keener awareness of His providence. Such knowledge "reveals His power and might, blessed be He, and that should be investigated." We are obligated to pursue every field of study which enables us to recognize "the nature of the universe . . . for it is all God's work . . . and thereby one recognizes his Creator." The great builders of science were not of the Jewish faith, but this did not deter Rabbi Judah. The quest for truth must not halt at denominational frontiers. God is the source of all our wisdom and knowledge, and He does not differentiate among persons on the basis of their religious affiliations. As Rabbi Judah put it, the wisdom "of the nations" is also from God; it is He "Who imparted to them of His wisdom." There might be objections to studying under teachers who are hostile to the religious life. The personal ties formed between teachers and students are powerful; such teachers may exert subtle influences, to undermine a student's faith. No such objections exist, however, to the more impersonal act of studying the writings of such men; and books of science and philosophy should be studied freely, regardless of the doctrine they teach.

One cannot fortify one's religious faith by avoiding the views which are hostile to it. It is, above all, wrong to reject wholesale the writings of men because in some details they are antagonistic to certain of our deeply cherished beliefs, when those same writings also offer us so much that is good and true. The Greek philosophers, Rabbi Judah pointed out, often carry reason beyond the scope of its competence, and many of their teachings are opposed to our religious tradition. Yet on other matters, vital in our tradition, they offer us valuable reinforcements. Even when they contradict our religious tradition, however, it is helpful to know their views. We truly defend our faith when we know its adversary and overcome his challenge, not by shutting our eyes to his existence.

Rabbi Judah challenged, however, the thesis of rationalism —that there is no more in the universe than could be seen with the eyes of the intellect, and that our sciences and the philosophies we build on them give us infallible truth. The reality which underlies all existence is far vaster than any formulae we may draw up to interpret it. The ultimate truth about the universe cannot be grasped by our mortal minds. Science is therefore always a relative knowledge, good as far as it goes, but we must ever be aware that as we continue our quest for truth there will come ever newer discoveries, ever newer interpretations, ever "newer truth." The falsehoods of today are the "truths" of yesterday, and today's truth may well turn out to be tomorrow's falsehood.

Rabbi Judah pointed to the revolution in astronomical knowledge in his own time, referring clearly to the new theories of Copernicus. "One who is the founder of the new astronomy has come and he proposed a new conception, and he has disproved everything that the early astronomers understood as the interpretation of the courses of stars and planets and heavenly phenomena." And is the new astronomy the end of the road, the final truth? Not at all. The very author of the bold new doctrine concedes in his writings that "he cannot explain everything." Indeed, how could we expect science to yield us absolute truth? Every step by which it proceeds is based on certain basic assumptions, on "first postulates," and what are these but generalizations based on the functioning of objects in the physical world, *as it appears to us*. That is not the road to unerring truth.

Science is a valuable tool to know the physical universe, but there it halts. It can probe into the universe as a given fact, to unravel the detailed procedures by which it operates. It can describe what exists. It cannot give us the answer to the deeper riddles the heart seeks to have resolved. It cannot enlighten us as to the ultimate source or purpose of our lives or of the universe which is our home. It cannot deal with the non-material reality which has its being side by side with the material.

The study of the natural order is "like a ladder by which to climb to the wisdom of the Torah." But how many students of science climb the ladder to its summit? How many proceed from the study of nature to what lies beyond nature? Rabbi Judah criticized the tendency among men of science to act on the notion that the natural order exhausts the meaning of reality. Nature, Rabbi Judah expounded, is not a final cause, nor a self-sufficient realm of being. The world which comes within the scope of the scientist's investigation, a world where there are only natural phenomena transpiring by natural necessity is only a dimension of existence. It is only a phase of larger reality in which existence is grounded.

The reverence for nature as though it were a self-sufficient realm of being, Rabbi Judah denounced as idolatrous. The natural order, in all its many attributes that elicit our admiration, remains dependent on God; He is the source of its being and it is to Him that our gaze of reverent gratefulness must be ever turned. "When men do not pass from the realm of nature to revere God, as they ought to, but remain within the realm of nature, without contemplating Him who wrought and perfected it all . . . then we have here a form of idolatry."

FROM THE WORLD OF THE CABBALAH

Rabbi Judah placed the natural order within the context of the workings of divine creation. It is God Who endowed the qualities of each being to behave as it does in relation to other beings. The universe, moreover, is not completely determined; and the phenomena of the universe are not exclusively the result of the workings of natural necessity. For God's relation to the world, taught Rabbi Judah, is not, as Aristotle pictured it, a necessary consequence of His being. It is a relationship of free grace. He willed creation, and He willed the character of existence as well as the goals and purposes which it is seeking to realize. Above the realm of nature and natural necessity, which reason can investigate, there is a realm of freedom, where God retains the initiative and when it seems good to Him, He injects Himself into human life to continue His providential ordering of existence.

As an illustration of God's continuing activity in the universe, Rabbi Judah cited the ceaseless urge to unity which dominates all creatures. One of its most glorious manifestations is the love between the sexes, which is the foundation of marriage and the family. All this for Rabbi Judah was but the continuing expression of God's presence. On the natural level, distinct lives would remain isolated from each other. The subtle force working against separatism and striving for oneness reveals a universe that is more than a soulless mechanism. It reveals a universe in which God is an ever present activating agent, stirring people toward goals He meant them to reach.

The most significant expression of divine freedom, transcending the realm of nature, is God's self-revelation to man, by illuminating prophets and teachers with the truths about His own being and about the order of life which is to constitute their highest good. These are embodied impressively in the sacred Scriptures, and to these a man must turn. He cannot live by reason alone. Reason's fruits must be supplemented by those of revelation. In addition to science, we must base life on the Torah and the divine commandments.

Reason will guide a man in the affairs of this world but that is its limit. It does not shed enough light to illumine our path toward God. The most important knowledge a man needs is how to live, and that cannot be attained by purely rational aids alone. "There isn't the power in the light which is reason to illumine the path on which one must walk toward his Creator. . . . This matter is above the competence of reason." We are saved from total ignorance on these matters through the fact that the "Lord revealed His ways to Moses and then to the prophets and our wise men have received the tradition from them and conveyed it to us. . . ."[2]

Chapter 3

ON REACHING FOR THE ULTIMATE

RABBI JUDAH DENOUNCED the claim that the study of science and philosophy is the supreme end of man's existence on earth. "The philosophers," Rabbi Judah writes, "have challenged the study of the Torah and the commandments. . . . According to them a person would achieve more significant results by devoting himself to the study of the spheres and the separate Intelligences, for they believe that man's true end lies in the comprehension of these matters. As to the immortality of the soul, they teach that it is the intellectual potentialities realized by a person in his lifetime which survive after his death. But know that this is an outright denial of our faith. Add to it the fact that it is against the intelligence, and common sense cannot entertain it at all."

Rabbi Judah's objections to these theories concentrates on showing that they are intellectually untenable. He does not content himself with quoting texts to prove them heresy. The acquisition of a valid body of concepts in metaphysics, Rabbi Judah argued, is a most difficult undertaking. It promises success only to a chosen few, and what of the rest of humanity? Can it be that God created a world and placed great multitudes of people into it, but doomed the preponderant numbers among them to live and die in ignorance, without the possibilities of attaining the true end of their existence? Man's end, according to them, "cannot be achieved except by one or two in a generation. Does the world then exist only for them?"

The promise of immortality offered by the philosophers, even to the chosen few, is a spurious immortality. For man is not a bundle of concepts, and to assure us that the concepts we have acquired will survive after death is little comfort to a person. It is like telling him that some of his other possessions will survive him. "If as they say survival applies only to the acquired intellect, then there is no survival for man himself. The intellect which he has cultivated is like his other possessions, his home, his wealth, his children, for these concepts are not man's essence."

The philosophers, moreover, Rabbi Judah argued, have divorced religion from morality. A person can develop intellectually, without rising in moral stature. Yet from the standpoint of what the philosophers call religion, all that counts is intellect. Thus according to them "one who has acquired concepts has achieved immortality, even though his deeds are despicable and despised by the Lord." Indeed, one may even rise to an intellectually profound conception of God's role in creation, without attaining piety, without learning to love or to fear Him. From Rabbi Judah's point of view, such a person ranked lower than the most ignorant soul that, despite its ignorance, feels a deep love for God. "One who has wisdom without piety is all the more reprehensible because of his wisdom, since he comprehends his Creator without fearing Him."

Rabbi Judah shared the notion which was commonly believed in his time that the heavenly bodies control the destinies of men on earth. At the same time he denounced the veneration for the spheres and the stars, which led the philosophers to regard a knowledge of these bodies as the highest knowledge that a man must seek. The notion derived from Aristotle for whom the spheres were living beings, who drew their power from the first Cause, through the separate Intelligences or souls, but who then exerted the influences that keep the universe going. Our own earth was the last in this series of spheres, and it was steered by its intelligence, the Active Intellect. Rabbi Judah disputed all this as pure mythology; a mythology, moreover, in which God is made remote from this universe, in which a series of intermediaries are placed between Him and creation. "Pay no attention to the opinion of the philosophers who said that the sun and the moon are living, intelligent beings, for all this is nonsense. They are physical objects."

Rabbi Judah scoffed at the predominance assigned by the Aristotelians to the Active Intellect. The Active Intellect was made almost sovereign over our earth below, as a kind of divine viceroy deriving his powers from God but then exercising them on his own right throughout earthly existence. Rabbi Judah derided this as pure invention, a theory without foundation. There may be invisible powers through whom God does His work, but it is in God that all such powers have their being, and whatever transpires in nature or in history, in any portion of cosmic life, is the direct offspring of His design and the result of His will.

The spheres have no special closeness to God. They are part of God's creation, endowed with specific functions, as are all other creatures. It is a mighty fine thing to study the heavenly bodies, but the knowledge so acquired is no more exalted than any other kind of knowledge. "Whoever comprehends in the spheres matters hidden from other people is like one who attains skill in carpentry in a measure beyond what other people can do."

Surely there is no reason to exalt the spheres above man. The spheres are a means to an end; they serve to promote the processes of the universe. Man, on the other hand, is the end of creation since all else was made for him. And although man "is a bodily creature, nevertheless, because of the divine image in him . . . even the angels are inferior to him."[3]

Rabbi Judah then launched his criticism at the most crucial doctrine of the Aristotelians—the conception of God. For the rationalists the ultimate core of all existence was reason. God was for them the absolute Intellect, engaging solely in His own eternal self-contemplation. Proudly aloof from the world, and beyond involvement in mundane events, He performed His role in the universe, as the source of all its motions and actions, through a series of intermediaries, through the "Intelligences." But He performed this role through no exercise of will or direct action. The Intelligences, and in turn all beings below them, over whose destinies they presided, moved and acted by being drawn toward God, in an inevitable response to His perfection. As a lover is drawn to his beloved, so do all beings in the universe feel drawn to God, and this all pervasive excitation produces all the mutation of events which goes on in the world.

Rabbi Judah challenged all this. It was to him a kind of mythology, an idolatrous cult built around the deification of reason. The identification of God with reason was a limitation upon God. Reason, he held, was only a phase of existence; and to identify God with reason is as blasphemous as to identify Him with body. Did not the Cabbalah list *hokmah* and *binah*, "wisdom" and "understanding," in the structure of the divine *sefirot?* These are expressions of reason. Yet they are seen as emanations, or creations of God, rather than elements in His essence.

The intellect is like all other existences in nature, a product of God's actions, and not an aspect of His essential self. God's knowledge is not included in His being, as He is in Himself. It is His expression, His action, part of the panorama of objective existence, which He begets by His creative acts. God's essence, however, is altogether boundless, and incomprehensible. It must forever remain so, "for we cannot conceive God perfectly, in accordance with the true essence of His glory; and this is so because of the imperfections in all created beings."

Did the conception of God's total incomprehensibleness make Him unreal? Rabbi Judah denied this, citing an analogy which was popular with the Cabbalists. The real remains real even though we cannot define it. The human soul for instance, cannot be defined by us, but its reality is beyond question. God is simple, eternal, absolute Being, beyond all limitations, while every attempt to define His essence would be to limit Him. But being aware of God's incomprehensibleness, we may yet feel profoundly His reality. "And if it be said, since His essence is neither body nor mind, then what is His essence? Our answer will be: 'What about man's soul? Can a person discern its true essence?'"

It was in the name of the identification of God's essence with reason that the rationalists had proclaimed the impossibility of God's direct concern with the events of mundane life. A deed is first born in the mind. It is an element of knowledge before it can be brought into objective existence. But how can we assume that God would involve Himself in mundane events which are of fleeting duration? Only eternal and unchanging ideas might be associated with the mind of God. The destinies of particular individuals which fluctuate with time and circumstance cannot be within God's concern. Their careers must therefore be presumed to be governed by the workings of chance and not by divine providence.

This was also the reasoning of the rationalist theologian Levi ben Gershon in arguing against God's authorship of miracles. God cannot initiate changes in the order of nature, for all such changes would have to begin as ideas in the mind of God, and we cannot associate God with what is transitory, being one thing now and something else again at another time.

All these problems disappear, Rabbi Judah argued, the moment we reject the straight-jacket of the Aristotelian formula. God's essence, he expounded, "is not knowledge, and thus we need no longer be troubled that as His knowledge changes, His essence will be involved in change.... And this is the way of life that every Jew ought to acknowledge and believe in, and he should not go in the crooked paths they have lately devised.... A change in His will is not a change in His essence, even as any of His diverse acts do not involve a change in Him...."

Rabbi Judah was not disturbed that miracles would introduce an element of anarchy in the universe. He attacked those who taught a doctrine of total determinism, to whom the life of the universe was governed solely by the laws of natural causality. The doctrine of determinism is based on the conviction that the process of existence is an orderly process, and order implies uniformity. But, as Rabbi Judah insisted, we do not deny order in the universe by affirming God's continuing concern with cosmic life. The belief in miracles merely implies a modified conception of order. For miracles are not capricious interruptions of the flow of existence. They follow a logic of their own. There is a realm of the natural and a realm of the supernatural. Both are part of one plan, but each follows its own distinctive path. The natural requires a time element for an event to transpire; particular substances can act only in a circumscribed fashion. None of these limitations exist in the realm of the supernatural. But both are phases of the one design through which God performs His purposes. "The realm of nature is linked with the realm above nature, whence miracles come."

The world of the rationalists, moreover, had its own contradictions, Rabbi Judah added. If God Who is the first Cause is identified with a particular essence, reason, how can physical matter, a radically different essence, arise from His actions? It was one of the assumptions of Aristotle that there must be a correspondence between cause and effect, that the effect cannot differ in its essential nature from the cause which produced it. The emergence of a concrete world of material objects therefore remains a freak appearance, which cannot be accounted for by the workings of the well-established laws of causality. "All this arises," continued Rabbi Judah, "if we assert this postulate that His essence is simple Intellect. But if we assert that His essence is simple Being, then . . . even physical creatures can arise from Him, because He is simple undifferentiated Being, and from His existence derive all existences. Simple, undifferentiated Being, whose essence transcends everything in our experience, may yet be ample enough to beget the realm of the physical as well as the realm of intellect. The moment, however, we have identified God with one of these realms, the other is left dangling in air, its roots detached from the creative source of all life, and excluded from the process by which beings arise in the hierarchy of existence.[4]

In reaching for life's ultimate reality we must go beyond nature, and beyond reason. We shall find it only as we turn to the ineffable oneness of God through whom all things arise and have their being.

CHAPTER 4

THE AUTONOMY OF FAITH

THE RELIGIOUS LIFE, as Rabbi Judah saw it, is an autonomous enterprise of the human spirit. It rests on three articles of faith. The first is divine providence, the faith "that God looks after the creatures on earth below, and not, as the heretics say, that the Lord is withdrawn from the world." The second is God's omnipresence, that "all things are in the hands of God and there is nothing outside Him. This is the real significance of believing in the existence of God. For surely every one believes that there is a God, but it is important to renounce the notion that God is not in everything, and that it is possible to withdraw from His jurisdiction." The final element of our faith is revelation, that God "speaks to man and has given him the the Torah. This is the belief that the Torah is divine."

Faith in these aspects of God's relation to man is the greatest demand of religion. And it is this faith which yields man the greatest rewards. It gives one the sense of assurance and inner fortitude. It places one's being firmly on the ground of life, and lifts him above the flux of time and circumstance. It makes him poised, joyful, confident, serene. He enjoys paradise in this world. For that is paradise—a state of "serenity and joy, the absence of outer pressures and sadness." Through faith he becomes truly free, since he becomes indifferent to the opinions of other men. Thus "he cleaves unto God, and then he has renounced the authority of other masters."

Religion may gain from the fruits of intellectual development, but it is not dependent on it. Religion is not a creation of our reason and its existence is not based on preliminary achievements in science and metaphysics. Religion has as its aim the deepening of our relations with God; it seeks to unite man with the divine source of his life. This aim it can pursue directly, without the mediation of science and metaphysics. It has its own source of truth—divine revelation or prophecy. It has its own path toward the goal it seeks—the study of the Torah and the performance of its precepts.

Rabbi Judah discussed the phenomenon of prophecy in only a sketchy fashion. It is clear, however, that he did not share the Maimonidean insistence that intellectual perfection is one of the prerequisites of prophecy. Prophecy is a "pouring in" upon the prophet of truth from its divine source. It is God's intervention in history, to offer man guidance toward his true destiny. In its highest form, prophecy is an intense, a mystical experience in which the prophet cleaves directly to God, and in this act of union there occurs the illumination by which the prophet sees the truth.

The Torah is the ripened fruit of this process of prophetic inspiration. Its highest achievement is the work of Moses, who was the greatest of the prophets. He laid down the fundamental beliefs and practices which were to establish a way of life for all time to come. The prophets who followed him represented a less creative level of prophecy. They dealt with the particular events in the history of their own time. But taken in its entirety the Torah is the principal means of steering man toward his good. It is the soul's answer to its endless seeking for a divine habitat. For the Torah derives from God; it is the pattern of higher wisdom, which God also embodied in the creation of the universe. And by studying and practicing what is prescribed in the Torah, we can achieve closeness to God, and raise life to its highest perfection. Through the Torah man becomes Godlike—to the extent that a creature can ever resemble its Creator.

Rabbi Judah rejected the view that the Torah was a purely human work, that the moral code was conventional in origin, and utilitarian in purpose. The assumption that the Torah is a purely human work, Rabbi Judah argued, would render life quite irrational. Everywhere throughout the universe we find design and order. Indeed, by contemplating the purpose and order in the universe, we affirm that this is a universe wrought and sustained by God. But if the Torah which teaches us the indispensable discipline for the stable and just order of human relations were only the work of the private reason of individuals, then the plan of creation would have been gravely defective. While providing the means for the perfection of every other creature, it would have failed to provide the means for the perfection of man, the most exalted and the noblest of creatures in the universe. The private discretion of individuals is too uncertain and variable a phenomenon to have depended on it for a knowledge of that truth by which alone man may vindicate his own life, as well as that of the rest of creation.

The divine character of the Torah is also supported by the nature of the intellectual process. According to the philosophers the transition of the potential reason to the actual reason is effected by God's principal intermediary in governing our world, the Active Intellect. We may ignore their notions about the Active Intellect, Rabbi Judah explained, for "we believe that God creates all things; not as they assert, that the Active Intellect performs these things, as one of the angels." What is significant, however, is their admission that a being who transcends man, in whom reason exists in all its fullness, without potentialities, must effect the transition in the human intellect from the potential to the actual. If this is true about the private reason of an individual, it must certainly be true of that reason which bears on the collective human community. "This necessarily proves conclusively that God inspires the collective reason which is the Torah, for the Torah represents influences of reason which bear on the collectivity, insofar as it is a collective."

We cannot assume that the moral code is merely a social convention, argued Rabbi Judah, for the rudiments of the moral system are discernible even in nature. Certain members of the animal kingdom, as the Talmud observed, exhibit some of the moral restraints which the Torah demands of man. The cat exhibits forms of modesty; the ant shows respect for the possessions of others; and the dove behaves with restraint in its sexual life. This suggested for Rabbi Judah that the roots of morality run deep into the nature of existence and are not merely the result of a human arrangement, which is relative to the culture prevailing at a given time.

It is not true, Rabbi Judah argued, "that robbery is evil because otherwise people would swallow each other alive, and that modesty is only a matter of respect and that a code of sexual behavior is only a convention, to keep people from promiscuity. It is not so at all. For if that were so, these virtues would not have arisen in the animal kingdom. This should prove conclusively that the moral virtues are not merely the result of a consensus among men, as some people have assumed. But the evil actions are intrinsically evil and the good actions are intrinsically good. . . ."

Rabbi Judah taught a doctrine of natural law. The principles of equity necessary to order human relations have been firmly planted by God in our common awareness of what is just. They are rooted in the underlying rationality which inheres in man, and it is independent of Scriptural imperatives even as it is independent of changes in culture. It is only for the doctrines which guide us toward God that we are dependent wholly on Scripture. Our reason may grope toward some of those doctrines but it can never achieve them in full clarity.

Rabbi Judah dismissed the objection that the commandment, being a bodily act, can have no effect on the soul. Because man's nature includes a physical element, the Torah also offers itself through a physical element. Its core of inner meaning is embodied in the commandments, which are executed by means of physical action. The disembodied meaning, functioning as an abstract idea, would be ineffective in reaching a bodily creature, who lives not only by reason but also by action. The allegorizing of the commandments on the grounds that physical action carries no vital significance for the spiritual man was

FROM THE WORLD OF THE CABBALAH

for Rabbi Judah a misinterpretation of the Torah as well as of human nature; it was an unwarranted disrespect "for the physical man." The Torah may be compared to a person, whose divine image is carried by a physical body. "The Torah itself, in its highest attributes, is similarly dependent on and carried by physical things, the commandments."

Rabbi Judah considered the scope and purpose of the individual commandments in the Torah. Some of his interpretations offer brilliant insights into the nature of the religious process and its role in human existence. His doctrine of prayer, for instance, is as penetrating an analysis of this fundamental institution in religion as is to be found anywhere in religious literature. The function of prayer and of the act of worship generally, he explained, is to prepare man to be a proper recipient of the divine beneficence. God's grace is ever directed to fulfill and to uplift and to bless His creatures, but only when we are deeply aware of our insufficiency and incompleteness and our need for Him, will we be properly attuned to receive His blessings. The man who lives by the illusion of his sufficiency has shut the door upon God's beneficent help; he has alienated himself from the flow of His goodness. The dynamics of new growth, the process of becoming in which we move to new levels of character and faith, is set in motion in the moments when we sense our acute need, our deficiency, and when our whole being goes out in intense yearning. That is the function of worship—it articulates our deficiency and deepens our sense of dependence on God. Thus the gap between man and God is bridged, and we are set in readiness to receive what the Lord is ever seeking to bestow on us.

It may be instructive likewise to cite Rabbi Judah's interpretation of the Sabbath. The Sabbath, Rabbi Judah explained, seeks to make us aware of the perfection of the world. It is meant to overcome the notion, fostered by the impressive range of our own achievements, the fruit of our own toil and ingenuity, that man himself is the source of whatever good he enjoys in the world. Thus is the perfection of the world, the

FROM THE WORLD OF THE CABBALAH

grandeur and glory which inheres in it, as a divine creation, obscured. On the Sabbath day man's initiative over the world, his manipulations of it, halt, and thereby we are called on to contemplate the universe as it is, without our "improvements" on it. A vital reminder is thus established to make us ever conscious of the perfection in God's work, this vast world, which is our home, even apart from man-made "additions" or alterations of it.

The highest significance of the commandments, however, Rabbi Judah insisted, is not in the specific benefits which each contributes to human life. Rabbi Judah objected to the "natural" explanations of the commandments as proposed by Maimonides. All commandments, regardless of their specific character, represent, as the Cabbalah taught, a device for lifting man out of the natural order toward the divine; they transcend utilitarian considerations. Their chief significance is in their linking man with God, which is the highest end of human existence.

Even the purely ethical commandment has not exhausted its function in the improvement of human relations. It has brought man nearer to God, since all commandments emanate from Him. The commandments are indeed patterns by which we may imitate God in our own behavior. Each commandment forges stronger the bond between man and God, and that is its highest service to human life.

If some commandments baffle our understanding, that is no reason for questioning their validity. Have the rationalists been able to account for everything in nature? Why should they be so impatient with elements of the Torah which they do not understand? It is enough to know that "all commandments represent a divine wisdom. Thus did the Lord ordain them, as is necessary for man, not as human intelligence dictates but in accordance with the order established by God in His wisdom. Therefore cleaving to the commandment is cleaving to the divine higher wisdom, and thus one achieves union with God, blessed be He."[5]

[120]

FROM THE WORLD OF THE CABBALAH

Rabbi Judah considered the objection which students of philosophy had often raised against the Torah—that its language is anthropomorphic. It refers to God in corporeal terms and endows Him with attributes and emotions which are part of mortal life. Maimonides had met the issue in his theory that the language of anthropomorphism was the language suited for the undeveloped multitude, who could not help but conceive God imperfectly. The very same Scriptural passages spoke, however, in different terms to the cultivated. For them God was without all attributes, without all emotions. And Maimonides called on people to discipline themselves to thinking of God as absolute Being, without attributes, without emotions, without any aspects of corporeality.

Rabbi Judah objected to making the Torah one thing for the masses and another thing for the educated, select few. Such a distinction offended his sense of the universal dignity of all men. It also carried a slur on the Torah whose obvious meaning was thus shown to convey an imperfect doctrine, a doctrine fit for the ignorant, for women and children, as Maimonides in one instance described it.

Rabbi Judah had another answer to this question. On the one hand many of the so-called anthropomorphisms are not anthropomorphisms at all, Rabbi Judah taught. When Scripture asserts that Moses ascended to God, it means that Moses "emancipated himself from the physical to attach himself to the spiritual." The reference to a physical organ designates the function performed by the organ, not the organ itself, which is only a tool. When Scripture speaks of the "eyes" or "ears" of God, it means to suggest that God knows what goes on in the universe. But God is surely without physical organs.

Physical objects are only the materialization of spiritual realities. In man, the spiritual has become materialized, while in God, it remains as a disembodied spiritual essence.

Some Scriptural passages were indeed anthropomorphic, and some ascribed positive attributes to God. But here Rabbi Judah offered the thought that God works on people in accordance with their spiritual development. For some God is indeed anthropomorphic; He is experienced in human form. And Scripture speaks of God *as men experience Him*. For Maimonides all references to God which imply corporeality are a compromise of the truth, aimed to make the text more comprehensible to the multitude of the people in later generations who were to live by it. Rabbi Judah, on the other hand, regarded these references as reflecting the limited comprehension of the Biblical characters whose experiences were a medium of transmission of divine truth. Even as light is refracted by the medium through which it passes, so is truth affected by the human agents through which it must be conveyed.

It is not strange that Scripture should convey, instead of the whole truth, a human conception of the truth. For man is the center of the end of all existence. God invited him to pronounce the proper names upon all creatures, as Scripture relates, thus implying that the human perspective was to be employed in appraising the various objects that are to be found in the universe. The characterization of God is no exception to this principle. It must similarly proceed from man's perspective; and it must be in relation to man's general outlook, to his level of perfection. God's essence we can never know. We can only know Him by his work, as we experience Him at any particular time; and any experience is always relative to the person involved in the experience. God reveals Himself to man in accordance with his capacities to comprehend Him. Moses, for instance, who had achieved a higher level of perfection, conceived God as incorporeal. Isaiah, on the other hand, who was below Moses in spiritual development, thought of God in terms of corporeality. Both were true conceptions in the sense that they each reported an authentic experience. God revealed Himself to each of them in accordance with their respective qualifications.

The anthropomorphisms of the Bible are true then, but in a relative sense. They reflect the relative spiritual maturity of men. "The Blessed be He is characterized by epithets in accordance with the experiences of those who so characterize Him. And it is certainly true that He will act on people in accordance with their preparation to be the recipients of such action. But there is no change or corporeality or emotion in God...."

In the light of this principle Rabbi Judah met the challenge of every passage in the Bible as well as in the Talmud where God is spoken of in terms of corporeality. Thus he treated the story of God's descent at Sinai. "Designations are determined by man, and therefore why be surprised because it is written, 'And the Lord descended.' From man's perspective it says that He descended or came, for thus did he experience God's glory—for man, He came to Mt. Sinai. And since thus did man experience God, there is no difficulty. This is the mighty principle on which we build great matters—that God is experienced in accordance with the recipient of the experience.... And if you say, 'But according to reason we cannot speak of God as descending,' consider then that man is not wholly a creature of reason."

Similarly he met the issue of passages which ascribe emotions to God. Thus he wrote concerning the verse "And it grieved Him in His heart" (Gen.6:6): "All these statements are not in accordance with His essence, for in His essence God is in His same condition and dignity. He was only conceived in this manner by man. When the generation of the flood did not do God's will and then He sought to destroy them, God was conceived in sadness.... The conclusion of the matter is that there is no reason to reject such statements because they imply corporeality. All of it is written from man's point of view."

The Torah exists in two forms, the written and the oral. The written Torah is the direct fruit of the prophetic experience, but it depends for its completion on the oral Torah. For the prophetic utterance is general and universal, and it depends on the work of reason to particularize it, to elucidate it, to apply it, to draw therefrom its many varied implications.

Rabbi Judah cited the observation of the Talmudists that

many works of God depend for their final perfection on the contribution of the human factor. Thus the wheat one gathers from the field will not reach its finally perfect state until man has ground it into flour. The prophetic utterance is a kind of natural product still waiting for its final perfection upon a rational examination by men of reason. "The Torah came into the world, as all natural objects, which did not come into the world completely clarified, but which depend on the rational human being to clarify them." That work of final clarification is the oral Torah, the vast literature of the Talmud.

The oral Torah includes certain enactments of the rabbis. Some of these are precautionary measures intended to safeguard various prescriptions in the written Torah. There are, however, some altogether new enactments, such as the establishment of the festival of Hanukkah. Wilful changes in the Torah, which are not inspired by special circumstances, would of course be objectionable. These enactments are, however, a response to definite historical circumstances, and they are fully justified. Contemporary rabbinic authorities, according to Rabbi Judah, continued to have the prerogative of meeting historical circumstances with special enactments, without being bound by precedent for their views.

Indeed it is perfectly proper when executing such enactments, Rabbi Judah explained, to offer the customary benediction thanking God for having ordained them. These enactments of the oral Torah are identical in spirit with the mandates of the written Torah. They constitute one process, one endeavor to perfect man. And it is God who conferred wisdom upon the rabbis and inspired them to act in response to the changing needs of human life. For divine inspiration is a continuous process, and it was not exhausted in the historical moment when Moses proclaimed the law to Israel. The relationship of the rabbinic enactments to the written Torah is similar to the relationship of natural phenomena to divine providence. "No person will say that what nature has wrought is not of God, for He, may He be blessed, ordained nature.

And this is similar. What the rabbis enacted is entirely of God, who arranged for the rabbis to act with their reason on whatever measures required enactment. . . ."

The rabbinic supplement, added to clarify the written Torah, was necessarily a body of oral tradition; and it is appropriately designated as an "oral Torah." For the implementation of a universal doctrine is an endless process. The fundamental principles can be itemized and recorded, while the applications of these principles are infinite. "The written Torah embodies commandments which are like the foundation and root; and the root and foundation may be fully stated. But the oral Torah which derives from the written Torah . . . for this there is no conclusion or end."[6]

Chapter 5

THE CABBALAH AND THE INTERPRETATION OF SCRIPTURE

RABBI JUDAH'S DOCTRINE of the Torah challenged every attempt of rationalists to differentiate its meaning into two levels, one for the common people, and another for the philosophically sophisticated. But Rabbi Judah taught a duality of his own. There was the physical word, the prescription for a physical act, but this was only the outer garment, an external shell within which is contained the precious essence, the divine, higher wisdom, the "soul" of the Torah. Rabbi Judah took sharp issue with the notion of Maimonides that while the basic elements in the Biblical Commandments have a purpose, detailed provisions may be arbitrary. For Rabbi Judah nothing is arbitrary. The "higher" reason behind the commandments is not always discernible on the surface; it is concealed in its outer garment. The divine reason permeates Scripture to the minutest detail. But as the soul shines through the body so does the divine reason shine through its outer garment, which is the physical word. The physical word takes on added sanctity because of the divine, higher reason which inhabits it.

Rabbi Judah quoted from the well-known passage of the Zohar "Woe unto the people who say that the Torah was merely concerned with telling of stories about this world. . . . That which is the essence of the Torah is clothed in these stories as a garment. Those who understand center their attention on the soul of the Torah. . . ." The comment of the Zohar speaks only concerning Scriptural narrative, but, Rabbi Judah adds, "the commandments are included in the pronouncement, for they cannot be in this material world, except within a physical body. . . . Although the entire content of the Torah is heavenly, it is placed within a physical garb. And as man comprehends the physical aspect of the Torah, it carries him over to the mystery which inheres in it, and it is as though man has become united with that divine wisdom."

What is the source of "mystery" which inheres in the Torah? It is explained by a number of Cabbalistic conceptions. The Cabbalists visualized creation as a chain of being that moves from the divine to the material. It is the materialization of a plan, of ideas. But ideas require a vehicle of language for their expression. The Hebrew language, as the language of the Torah, was also accepted therefore as the vehicle of creation. The *Sefer Yezirah* (Book of Creation), one of the earliest of Cabbalistic works, phrases it this way: "By means of the twenty-two letters, by giving them a form and shape, by mixing them and combining them in different ways, God made the soul of all that which has been created and of all that which will be. It is upon these same letters that the Holy One blessed be He has founded His high and holy name." And, so the Cabbalists assumed, if we but seek it, we may find "echoes" in the very structure of the Hebrew language which reveal its higher significance, a correspondence between words and letters and the most significant facts about God's creation.

The highest triumph of this doctrine of letters, as may be noted in the statement of the *Sefer Yezirah,* was centered in the verbalizations of the names of God. The various aspects of God's creative self are conveyed through the various names by which He is designated in Scripture. What is decisive in these names, according to the Cabbalists, is the configuration of letters by which each name is represented. "The entire universe," declared Rabbi Judah, "was created by His names." There was incidentally the fateful implication contained in this notion that man's invocation of the divine names would continue to exercise potency over creation, to effect changes in nature. This was to become a source of occult practices, of the pathetic

FROM THE WORLD OF THE CABBALAH

endeavor to control life's destiny through special incantations, especially of God's secret names. We have already noted that this was one of the ingredients out of which Jewish folk-lore created the *golem* legends, in which Rabbi Judah figured as the principal hero.

The words and letters of the Hebrew language take on added significance because each letter has a numerical equivalence. The first ten letters of the alphabet represent the numbers one to ten; the next nine letters, twenty to a hundred; and the final three letters, two hundred to four hundred. All other mathematical symbols are represented by a combination of those letters. Here the Cabbalists drew upon a doctrine which in its original formulation goes back to Pythagoras, that the highest reality in the universe is mathematical relationships, which are expressed in numbers. In Cabbalism this doctrine is transposed into the equivalence of the Hebrew letters. The translation of words and letters into their numerical symbols and the reverse translation of numbers into their language symbols becomes a source for the search of clues to the hidden mysteries about God and the universe.

The context in which these ideas operated was of course the doctrine that the Torah is the design of creation, the pattern of divine ideas which God embodied in the universe. Biblical narratives, the commandments, the lives of Israel's early heroes, the Temple and its furnishings, all are shown as embodying elements of this higher wisdom. In Rabbi Judah's writings the Talmudic text is treated similarly. A correspondence is shown to exist between the word and the higher meaning of which it becomes the symbol.

Many of these ideas are earlier than the Cabbalah. The Talmudists engaged occasionally in the interpretation of the Biblical text in symbolic terms, and in the transposition of words into their numerical equivalence. In the Cabbalah this method of interpretation is much more frequently employed, and understandably so. The elaborate theosophy of the Cabbalists was singularly missing in the revealed texts of Scripture. The Talmudic texts too were free of ideas that played so dominant a role in the Cabbalistic interpretation of Judaism. The very term *Cabbalah,* an oral transmission, was the Cabbalists' answer to this anomaly. The teachings of the Cabbalah were a secret doctrine, unsuited for the common masses of humanity, and they were transmitted as an oral tradition, until some of this higher wisdom was finally reduced to writing. The feeling that these ideas were esoteric, mysterious, and that the common run of humanity were unqualified to receive them, explains the reticence among Cabbalists when they speak of their favorite themes; they speak in hints rather than in explicit declarations. But it was only natural that they endeavor to find allusions and hints in the traditional texts of Judaism for their secret wisdom.

It was the conviction of the mystics also that our own very world is a divine expression, that God can somehow be recognized directly in the very being of the universe. The universe will reveal its higher dimension of meaning to illuminated minds that can look beneath appearances, that can penetrate the garment to see the reality within it. The discovery of parallelisms between nature and the higher wisdom of the Torah fitted in with the demands flowing from that conviction.

These were the common ideas among the mystics, and they were subscribed to in Christian no less than in Jewish circles. Thus Paracelsus, an older contemporary of Rabbi Judah and a spokesman of Christian mysticism declared: "If we wish to know the inner nature of man or his outer nature, we must pursue our explanation of nature on the foundation of the Cabbalah. For the Cabbalah opens up access to the occult, to the mysteries; it enables us to read sealed epistles and books and likewise the inner nature of men."

It may be instructive to cite some of Rabbi Judah's interpretations of Bible and Talmud which reveal this method of the Cabbalah. Rabbi Judah saw a correspondence between the ten *sefirot* which designate in the Cabbalah the varying levels of God's creative self, and the ten miracles which the Mishnah in Abot 5:4 lists as having occurred in the Temple. Creation in six days reflects an element of perfection in the world, for the number six is the simplest number, since it is the most readily divisible.

The Biblical preference for the number seven is explained on the theory that seven corresponds to the middle stratum of being which stands between the completely material and the completely spiritual. Four stands for the material, as is suggested by the four dimensions of the physical. Ten is the highest point in the numerical series and therefore symbolizes the divine. Seven is the median between four and ten, and fittingly stands for the universe as a whole, in which, as the *Sefer Yezirah* teaches, there are six directions, east, west, north, south, as well as height and depth, and in the center of which is the Holy Temple supporting the whole.

The middle number in a series was always regarded as specially sacred. In part this reflected the Aristotelian identification of the golden mean with the good. The middle element was also regarded as the mediator between the extremes and thus a crucial link in the continuity of life. The two tablets of the Law each carrying five of the ten commandments correspond to the two hands, each with its five fingers.

The numerical value of the Hebrew letters which spell Sinai, the desert on whose mountain God proclaimed the Law to Israel, is identical with that of the letters which spell *sulam*, a ladder. This suggests that as a person renounces the distractions of the world and makes himself as free as the desert, he has fashioned for himself a ladder by which to climb toward God. To the rabbinic suggestion that the Torah begins with the letter *bet*, because it stands for *braha*, blessing, he added that *bet* represents blessings not because it is the initial letter of the word *braha*; the Hebrew word *bukah*, which means a curse also begins with *bet*. But *bet* numerically stands for two, which begins plurality or amplitude, which is blessing.

FROM THE WORLD OF THE CABBALAH

The Biblical and Talmudic texts took on a new flexibility in these interpretations of the Cabbalists. Talmudic utterances which occasionally seem baffling to our understanding could often be given a symbolic interpretation, which made them into vehicles of profound ideas. Some of these texts had been occasionally cited for criticism by spokesmen of rationalism, or by Christian polemicists intent on proving the spiritual inadequacy of Judaism. The transposition of such an utterance into the higher meaning which it represented proved an effective weapon in defense of classic Jewish texts.

It was through this method of interpretation that Rabbi Judah met the challenge of Azariah dei Rossi's *Meor Enayim*. Those strange tales of the Talmud which often seemed to abound in so much fantasy and exaggeration were in truth parables of profound significance. Thus he denied that the story of the flea which supposedly killed Titus by entering his brain and boring in it for seven years was meant to be taken literally. The flea as a physical object is but a material expression of an immaterial essence or force. The copper beak and iron nails which one rabbi ascribed to the flea were only to suggest the severity of that essence or force. In the interval of seven years which elapsed between the burning of the Temple and his death, Titus suffered from a pressure on his brain, which finally brought on his death.

We cite one more instance of Rabbi Judah's method of interpretation. It illustrates the transformation of baffling prose into stirring poetry which Talmudic texts went through under the touch of his exposition.

There is a Midrash which teaches that the donkey on which Abraham rode on his way to Mt. Moriah in order to offer Isaac as a sacrifice to God was the same donkey on which Moses rode later on, and on which the Messiah is destined to ride when he makes his appearance in the world. It is a strange statement, but Rabbi Judah explained it ingeniously. The Hebrew word for donkey, *hamor,* is of the same root and is built

FROM THE WORLD OF THE CABBALAH

of the same consonants as the word *homer,* which means the *material.* Rabbi Judah suggested therefore that the Midrash really means to assert the similarity in spiritual stature between these three inspired leaders in Israel. For *hamor* was here a poetic allusion to *homer;* and to ride over it, means to master it. The Midrash thus teaches that those three men were equally the masters of the material world about them.[7]

CHAPTER 6

EDUCATION AND LIFE

THE RATIONALISM which affected the Jewish community was only in part the rationalism of the philosophers. Another variety of rationalism flourished in medieval Jewry, and it enjoyed a much wider following. This was the rationalism of Talmudic dialectics.

The prevalent fashion in the rabbinical academies which set the tone for Jewish culture generally was to pursue the keen analysis of Talmudic texts, with their commentaries and super-commentaries. Not merely the select few, but the common man as well, was given the goal of studying the Talmud. Its intricate discussions of civil law, of marriage and divorce problems, of ritual purity and Temple sacrifices, became the all-absorbing issues to which men gave their best intellectual energies. These questions themselves, moreover, were of only secondary interest. It was the play of intellect, the sharpness of analysis, the minute distinctions between minor points, the discovery and resolution of textual contradictions which was the heart of this enterprise.

Talmudic rationalism invaded even the elementary schools, and children of a tender age were introduced to the study of the Talmud, moving from the text to the commentaries and then to original feats of analysis. The justification for this procedure was that it sharpened the mind, and developed the students' intellectual powers.

The most gifted products of this educational system were men of high specialization who were at home in the most abstruse legal discussions of the Talmud, but who knew little of the inspired writings that comprise the other branches of

[133]

FROM THE WORLD OF THE CABBALAH

Jewish knowledge. By training, moreover, these men had developed the tendency to dialectics and casuistry. What they prized most was not characters refined by the moral preoccupations of the Bible, the simple disciplines enunciated in the Mishnah, or the affirmations of God in the works of pietists and mystics. They cared more for minds gifted in dialectical skill. Above all, the trouble with Talmudic rationalism was that it was another screen between man and God. The sharpening of the mind replaced the deepening of the love of God as the supreme end in man's life.

It may be significant to note that the emphasis on dialectics was a phase of medieval culture generally. Betraying its rationalist orientation, all medieval education had as its major goal the sharpening of the mind. As one historian put it, the "characteristic of the pedagogy of the Middle Ages, its mania, was the taste or rather passion for disputation." What the Talmud was in the rabbinical academies, the texts of Aristotle were for the Christian schoolmen.

The humanists challenged this over-concentration on dialectics. They regarded the poring over Aristotelian texts a sterile business. Reflecting the trend to mysticism, they preferred the Platonic philosophy, in which they saw a greater appreciation for the values of direct experience over those of the purely intellectual life. They showed a keen appreciation for the study of nature which was regarded as a faithful model of human behavior. This conception of nature derived from the notion emphasized by the mystics that nature was but the materialization of God's creative thoughts and that man was a microcosm, a miniature edition of the universe itself. The important pedagogic inference was drawn from this that education itself was to follow nature, grading subjects of study on the basis of the child's natural development.

We gain a glimpse into the reactions of the humanists to current education through the testimony of Peter Remus. "Gentlemen," he relates in a revealing personal note, "when I came to Paris, I fell among the subtleties of the sophists, and they taught me the liberal arts through questions and disputings, without showing me any other advantage or use. When I had graduated as master of arts, I . . . decided that these disputes had brought me nothing but loss of time. Dismayed by this thought, led by some good angel, I chanced on Xenophon and then on Plato and learnt to know the Socratic philosophy." "Liberal arts," Remus further declared, "should be kept relative to human life, and help men to think and act well, but schools teach subtleties useless in practice." These ideas are echoed by all the representative thinkers of the century. They reached their fullest maturity in the writings of Comenius, the father of modern education, who was born in Moravia in 1592, as Rabbi Judah neared the twilight of his own life.

Every resurgence of Jewish mysticism reacted against Talmudic rationalism. The Cabbalah disputed the conventional study of the Talmud which made the mental exercise of study an end in itself, and which missed the highest dimension of meaning in Talmudic texts—their more spiritual teachings of which the literal world was only a symbol. The Cabbalah became a popular movement in the guise of hasidism, and here we find outspoken criticism against the submergence of piety in dialectics. It is not surprising therefore that Rabbi Judah's polemic against rationalism should have extended to an attack against the rationalism built around the Talmud, advocating a reformation in Jewish education.[8]

Rabbi Judah launched his attack on the current practices in education on the ground that they were sterile and wasteful. The study of the Talmud was admittedly an important subject in the curriculum, but the casuistry with which the schools surrounded that study robbed it of all efficacy. Over-concentration on individual passages, by subjecting them to super-fine analysis through commentaries and super-commentaries, Rabbi Judah maintained, was an impediment to progress. It centered discussion on a particular text beyond its real importance, and thus impeded the necessary movement toward the mastery of the vast literature of the Talmud. Casuistry made for narrowness and ignorance, and doomed to futility the precious years that students invested in their quest for an education.

Rabbi Judah bemoaned this wastefulness with words full of pathos and grief. "The very beginning of their studies in Torah is such that the Torah cannot abide with them. . . . Woe unto us for the shame and the disgrace of it! We are inferior to all the generations past. And all because men follow the notion that they must sharpen the mind with casuistry . . . it is all utter folly. For all of us have seen the results of this sharpening of the mind. Our young men, when advanced enough in years to be ready for marriage, should surely have mastered any number of tractates of the Talmud, had they been given a good grounding in study from childhood on. As it is, they know nothing."

Rabbi Judah singled out the study of Tosefot for special censure. The Tosefot are a super-commentary on the Talmud, appearing on the margin of all standard editions of the Talmud. Occasionally offering a direct analysis of the Talmudic text, but more often analyzing the commentary of *Rashi,* the scholars who created the Tosefot usually raise all kinds of abstruse questions of law, and they proceed in involved dialectical analyses. By making the mastery of Tosefot an integral part of the study of any text, Rabbi Judah felt, the study of the Talmud was doomed to a fruitless play of the intellect, in which the Talmudic text itself was lost sight of. "The study of Tosefot," Rabbi Judah declared, "is responsible for the failure of education. As implied by the very meaning of the word, *Tosefot* are supplements to the text. Is it not more important, however, first to master the Talmudic text itself?"

Rabbi Judah rejected the claim that sharpening the mind has its justification in the development of a general skill, which might be transferred to other pursuits. There exists no occupation which calls for the type of dialectical acumen comparable to the casuistry practiced in the current study of Talmud. Moreover, if all one sought was an intellectual exercise, then it could be achieved more effectively through the study of a trade or a game of chess, which embody more wisdom and are surely more useful. Indeed, the skill achieved in mastering a trade is closer to the skill necessary to the genuine study of the Torah. Learning a trade disciplines one to seek the facts, to reach out for the truth. That is the spirit of the Torah, while the spirit of casuistry is an indifference to truth.

Rabbi Judah lashed out at the educators as well as the parents who allowed the current educational system to continue. He accused them of seeking not the truth but a means of ostentation. They were interested in developing "cleverness" and self-display but they were indifferent to facts.

"The principal attribute of Torah is the truth," Rabbi Judah expounded, "and it is this attribute which makes it eternal, for the truth does not change. . . . Therefore, how do people dare supplement the Torah with matters which are vain and false? . . . If a person spent all his time on Talmud, it would be a sufficiently serious departure from the path of the wise, the equitable path. But they do more grievously—they waste their days with these follies, which they call mind-sharpening 'pilpul.' Long ago I began to call on people to educate their children first in the Mishnah, as the foundation for further study, and then in the rest of the curriculum, as the rabbis ordained in their rules for the study of Torah. But I did not succeed, because of the intervention of men, sinners themselves and causing others to sin, who only aim to use the Torah for purposes of ostentation, and they kept the people from following my counsel. They told them that it is better for their children to study the *pilpul* of the *Gemara* and that through it they would rise to great heights. . . . And the little boys are taught to repeat like parrots, without the slightest notion of what it is all about. This is the practice of our lowly and mean generation that has gone off on crooked paths."

Current education, Rabbi Judah warned, is a training in confused and irresponsible thinking, which must necessarily lead to moral perversity as well. Turning directly to the students, Rabbi Judah pleaded with them: "I turn to you, dear students. . . . Do not waste your days with pursuits such as these, and do not labor in vain on what will yield you no reward. . . . You surely see that what you pursue is without substance. . . . And do not allow your teachers to assure you that there is value in what you are doing. For these assurances are false. . . . As the Lord liveth, one ought to rent his garments in grief over this condition as one does over a scroll of the Torah that has perished in the flames."

Rabbi Judah records the fierce opposition which he evoked by his attempt to eliminate "pilpul." He had written to the rabbis of Russia and Poland, inviting them to support his stand, but they turned a deaf ear to him. In his own community he attempted to introduce his own educational program, but the people resisted, and his efforts were to no avail.

Rabbi Judah accused the young students in the academies of being indifferent to real culture. He charged them with being careerists who studied for ulterior motives. The great ideal they were each concerned with was making an impression on some wealthy but ignorant family for the purpose of bringing about an advantageous marriage. Rabbi Judah charged that the degeneracy in the academies had caused the deterioration in the moral conditions of the people generally. A false standard had been projected and it led to a decline of character among the very highest classes in Jewish society. Rabbi Judah continued his great indictment by saying: "Any man of sense can see that this and nothing else is the cause of it."[9]

The sweeping criticism of Rabbi Judah finally directed itself at the rabbinate. Raised on a false system of education, the rabbis proved to be altogether unequal to the tasks which confronted them. Preaching, which for Rabbi Judah was endowed with the august function of influencing people toward the good life, was looked upon by the rabbis of his day as but another device for ostentation. The rabbis sought to impress people rather than to tell them the truth. Their words, too, were corrupted by casuistry. They revelled in the "clever" use of verses, without reference to the true meaning of a text. Indeed, many preachers spurned the obvious sense of a text because that was common knowledge. Ever seeking to be innovators, they did not hesitate knowingly to distort a verse, if it would only help them to impress people with their originality. Better to preach without a text at all, argued Rabbi Judah, than to indulge in a play of words, which preacher and public both know to be false. Rabbi Judah blamed this on the influence of the academies, "where all study is for purposes of ostentation." Rabbi Judah decried that so many unworthy men were being ordained in his day. The dishonor which they brought to the proud title of rabbi led to a general disrespect for the rabbinate, and for its authority in Jewish life. Rabbi Judah was especially concerned that even Palestine, which was then a vital center of Jewish piety and scholarship, was often guilty of those unworthy ordinations.[10]

Rabbi Judah was likewise critical of current methods in the teaching of the Bible. The practice was to parallel the study of the Pentateuch with the weekly cycle of Torah readings in the synagogue. The weekly portion was usually larger than what the child could cover during the week, and thus he was forced to skip in his studies. During the period of school vacations, moreover, whole sections of the Bible were omitted, since students resumed not where they had left off, but where the portion of the week occurred. This made for ignorance of large parts of the Bible, and for a confused understanding of the sections covered, which were necessarily, in many instances, studied out of context. The proper procedure in teaching Bible, according to Rabbi Judah, was to follow the text "in order, from beginning to end, and then to review it, until it has been fully mastered."

Another practice in the teaching of Bible which Rabbi Judah deplored was encumbering the text with the Rashi commentary. Rabbi Judah ascribed the origin of this practice to teachers in the villages, where texts were scarce, and they were happy to elaborate their lessons, so that they would not complete too soon the texts they had. The result, however, was to impede progress. The essential purpose of the study of Bible should be to master the Bible, and these diversions wasted time. Rabbi Judah's criticism did not stem from a lack of appreciation for Rashi as a Biblical commentator. Indeed, he thought highly of him. But he sought simplicity and directness in education, and he opposed the commentary especially when used by young children, as an unnecessary encumbrance and a distraction from the mastery of the text itself.[11]

Rabbi Judah decried especially the prevailing disregard for the nature of the child in the schools of his time. They ignored the need of adapting subjects of study to the capacities of the child. Their concern was to make haste, and they plunged the child into the most abstruse discussions, long before he was equipped for it. "Thus," Rabbi Judah writes, "a child of eight or nine commences the study of Talmud, but is this consistent with the state of his intelligence? Certainly the reasoning which is inconsistent with a person's capacities will not abide with him. . . . It is all futile when a child of immature years attempts to master what is not in accordance with the state of his intelligence."

The little boy learns to repeat what is drilled into him, but his heart is not in it, and he does not really comprehend it. "The little boy," Rabbi Judah wrote with scorn, "mouths mere words, but the semblance of the plain meaning he cannot understand. . . . Fortunately, the intelligence of the child develops of itself. Surely he cannot be benefited by the diet fed him, which is not fit for him, and which is not in accordance with the state of his intelligence. Indeed, if he were left without any instruction he could accomplish in a very short time all that he has received from the very start of his education."

Rabbi Judah called for a return to the standard indicated in the Mishnah, which he recognized as sound pedagogy, to commence the study of Bible at the age of 5, the Mishnah at the age of 10, and the Talmud at the age of 15. "This," Rabbi Judah wrote, "places the burden upon the child, as he can take it, in accordance with his nature. . . . The shepherds must lead the tender sheep at their own pace, not to strain them by driving them on a path which appears short, but is really long. Yea, it is not merely that this path is long. Travelling on that path, they will die without entering the mansions of Torah."[12]

Rabbi Judah emphasized the importance of repetition and review in learning. Only thus is knowledge fixed in the mind to become one's permanent acquisition. And only after several repetitions can the mind penetrate to the deeper wisdom which always eludes one on a first reading of a text or discussion. This was the secret of the great intellectual achievements of the early masters; they "were always reviewing their studies." In addition to the perversions wrought by casuistry, Rabbi Judah blamed the cultural decadence of his time to the insufficient emphasis on the importance of review in learning. The students learned a theme, and they quickly forgot it. They were like women who gave birth to children and were then bereaved of them.

Rabbi Judah criticized the practice of giving children long vacations between semesters. These vacations were unsupervised. The more zealous students generally used the free time of their vacations to study the legal codes. The others were left entirely on their own, with no specific program to guide them in their free time. Those vacations, Rabbi Judah charged, did not accomplish any positive good; they only caused students to forget what they had studied and they encouraged the mischief which always goes with idleness. Torah, Rabbi Judah declared, should be studied "daily, without interruption. . . . And they should study daily the basic principles of the law and then they should review the subject till they have mastered it. As for the study of codes . . . it is not a subject to be pursued by all. Only the more advanced students should take time out for the study of codes. For most, it suffices to study the principles of the law, and to review their studies, which is best of all."[13]

Another important aid in successful education, according to

FROM THE WORLD OF THE CABBALAH

Rabbi Judah, was group discussion. Students should form themselves into small study groups, especially for the purpose of reviewing their work. The challenge of diverse minds playing on one another produces alertness and concentration. It evokes more from the material under discussion as well as from the students. Based on the facts of the nature of a student, all those pedagogic aids must be utilized fully if education was to be efficacious in its mission.

The educational ideal advocated by Rabbi Judah was practical—to equip the child with the ideals and disciplines of Judaism, to develop within him a love for God and for the Torah. "A person," Rabbi Judah counselled, "should not devote himself to a subject of study, regardless of how exalted, if it is purely speculative and does not embrace some action." And this practical ideal should dominate the educational process from the very start.

The foundation of a sound Jewish education, according to Rabbi Judah, was the study of Hebrew language and grammar. Rabbi Judah took an interest in a progressive elementary school conducted in Posen by a certain Joseph Heilprin. There the children studied correct, grammatical Hebrew, in speech as well as in writing. Rabbi Judah encouraged this teacher to publish a primer in Hebrew grammar for young children. It appeared in Cracow in 1597, under the title *Em ha-yeled*, with a commendation by Rabbi Judah, which stated: "True and certain it is that a person is under a great religious commitment to train his child in the Hebrew language and grammar, as was done by our forefathers, may their memories be for a blessing." This was one subject which was generally neglected. Rabbi Hayim, a brother of Rabbi Judah, reports that Christians taunted the Jews over the barbaric Hebrew which they employed, and their total ignorance of the very rudiments of proper Hebrew style and grammar.[14]

The Bible was to be studied as the basic text enunciating the Jewish way of life. Rabbi Judah urged a practical emphasis in Biblical study. It should always endeavor to delineate the commandments, and to elucidate them. Thus would Biblical study direct itself toward a practical end. It would make for a better appreciation of the disciplines of Judaism, which are rooted in the teachings of the Bible.

The study of Bible should be followed by the study of Mishnah. The Mishnah should be the mainstay of the curriculum, since there we have an ordered statement of Jewish law. Rabbi Judah inspired the creation of the *Hebra Mishnayot*, the daily study group in Mishnah, which became one of the earliest and most successful projects in adult education. During the centuries that followed, in practically every synagogue in every village and town where Jews resided, the common people organized themselves into a study group for a daily session in the study of Mishnah. The institution began in Prague, and spread out at once to many other communities, as Yom Tob Lippman Heller, a disciple of Rabbi Judah, reports in the introduction to his commentary on the Mishnah.

The Mishnah was not a final code, of course. The fuller elaboration and clarification of the law was to be found in the Gemara, the explanatory supplement to the Mishnah, which follows it as a running commentary, and together with it, makes up the text of the Talmud. The Gemara was to be the next subject of study, and was to constitute the highest point in the curriculum. It was on the basis of the legal discussions in the Mishnah and the Gemara, Rabbi Judah demanded, that all new cases in law were to be adjudicated.

Rabbi Judah favored the study of the legal codes as a supplement to the Talmud, and as an aid in determining the law. But the code was never to be used by itself, as a final guide to action. His objection to the codes—he mentioned specifically the *Shulhan Aruk* by Rabbi Joseph Caro—was the fear of a mechanization in law. Because these codes omit the reasoning behind every legal decision, they reduce the law to a soulless formalism.

FROM THE WORLD OF THE CABBALAH

Rabbi Judah conceded that an individual rabbi's analysis of the Talmud may lead him to erroneous inferences, and thus to misinterpret the law. Nevertheless, there was no alternative. The rabbi must follow rigorously what his reason dictates, and what he comprehends in the Talmud. "Even when his reason and his understanding of the Talmud deceive him, he is beloved by God, if he determines the law in accordance with the promptings of his intelligence; and the only matter a judge can consider is what his own eyes behold. And this is preferable to deciding on the basis of one book without comprehending at all the reasoning behind things. One who does so is like a blind man feeling his way on the road."[15]

Rabbi Judah denounced the tendency of making education a class privilege. The Torah was meant to be the possession of all Israel, not only of the select few. Yet he noted that the prevalent system necessarily deprived the poor student of the opportunity to study. The schools were conducted as the private venture of some teacher, who cared only for the tuition fees, while the wealthy were only concerned with the education of their children. The model school which Rabbi Judah extolled, was the community school in which rich and poor were equally at home, regardless of tuition fees. It was the business of people of means to provide educational facilities for those who were not in a position to pay. Free of the many distractions which occupy the minds of wealthy children, the student of a poor home generally makes a superior scholar. The opportunity must therefore be given him to study. Indeed, his challenge and example will act as a spur to the children of the privileged homes, and thus prove an all-around boon to the cause of education.

Rabbi Judah entered his plea for educational reform to an obdurate community. Some of his pupils tried to carry on in their master's cause, but their words fell on deaf ears. The conventional school system was too firmly entrenched and it could not be shaken by his criticism.

FROM THE WORLD OF THE CABBALAH

Rabbi Judah was confident, however, that he would be vindicated in time, that eventually the Jewish school system would be reformed. He invoked his old theory of "creation through privation." Deficiency has a way of defeating itself in the end. When it proceeds far enough it begets an inevitable reaction. And when the decadence in education has reached its depths, a new creative surge will make itself felt among the people. They will at last destroy a perverse institution, and replace it with something better and nobler, in the image of his ideal.[16]

V

Judaism and Christianity

"Even if the words spoken are against one's faith and religion, do not tell a man not to speak and to suppress his words. Otherwise there will be no clarification in religious matters. On the contrary, one should tell such a person to say all he wants . . . and he should not claim that he would have said more had he been given the opportunity. . . . Thus my opinion is contrary to what some people think. They think that when it is forbidden to speak against religion, religion is strengthened. . . . But it is not so. The elimination of the opinion of those who are opposed to religion undermines religion and weakens it. . . . For every man of valor who wants to wrestle with another and to show his strength is eager that his opponent shall have every advantage to show his real powers. . . . But what strength does he show when he forbids his opponent to defend himself and fight against him?" (Rabbi Judah, in *Beer ha-Golah*, p. 151)

Chapter 1

THE HUMANISTS AND JUDAISM

AMONG THE MANY LEGENDS which were circulated about Rabbi Judah there is one which pictures him as the champion of Judaism in a thirty day debate against three hundred priests under the leadership of the Cardinal John Sylvester. It was Rabbi Judah, according to the story, who invited the disputations in an effort to expose the libels which were being circulated against Jews and Judaism. His memorandum which he addressed to the Prague Cardinal on the subject began with the challenging words: "I demand justice for my oppressed brethren." The Cardinal arranged the disputation and each day of the thirty day period he debated with a different group of ten priests.

The subjects on which he was challenged were: "Does the Talmud advise Jews to use the blood of Christians for Passover?;" "Are not the Jews guilty of crucifying Jesus?;" "Does not the Talmud advise Jews to hate Christians?;" "Why is the converted Jew despised among his former co-religionists?;" "Why do the Jews exalt themselves as the chosen people?" More than a hundred questions were addressed to Rabbi Judah and he answered them all patiently and to the complete satisfaction of the Cardinal and the priests, who then pledged him their friendship.

There is no evidence that such a debate ever occurred, but the folk-imagination was on solid ground in the essential ingredients out of which it built its story. One of the great themes in the writings of Rabbi Judah was the defense of Judaism against the challenge of Christianity.

FROM THE WORLD OF THE CABBALAH

The polemics between Judaism and Christianity were a natural development in an age which abounded in religious controversy. This was in a sense a by-product of the rise of mysticism. For the impact of mysticism on religion has always been to quicken and vivify its internal life. Every expression of religion assumed a new intensity as men saw in it a vehicle for the direct experience of God. Religion was taken with a profound earnestness and even minor differences of belief or practice became matters of great concern, eliciting heated debate. It is no wonder then that the age of mysticism also became the age of religious disputations. The Christian world was rocked by the controversies which precipitated the wars of the Reformation. Side by side with these controversies within Christendom there also raged another struggle, the struggle between Christianity and Judaism.

Christianity presented its challenge to Judaism in an active polemic literature which sought to demonstrate the truth of Christian doctrine. Its protagonists came from a variety of sources.

There were apostate Jews, those who could not withstand continued persecutions and solved their own problem through baptism.

Some of these converts tried to practice Judaism in secrecy; and thus there developed the problem of the *marranos*, people who lived ambiguous lives, professing Christianity while endeavoring in secrecy to practice Judaism. They were a problem to the Church as well as to the Synagogue. Some of these converts tried to make a complete break with their past; and to silence a troubled conscience they often turned against their former co-religionists, in whose continuing steadfastness they sensed a constant indictment of their own weakness. Among these converts were learned men, too, and they used their learning to disparage Judaism, and to urge those who still adhered to it to follow their example into freedom.

The attacks against Judaism came of course also from spokesmen for the Christian church. In 1559 all Hebrew books in Prague were seized, to be examined for possible anti-Christian reference. The contemporary historian, David Ganz, reports that not even a single prayer book was left and that the cantor had to chant the prayers orally. The Talmud was burned six times in the course of the 16th century, in 1553, 1555, 1559, 1566, 1592, and 1599. A Christian censorship of Hebrew books was introduced in 1562. In 1561 under the instigation of the Jesuits an order was issued forcing Jews to listen to Christian sermons, which disparaged their own faith and extolled the virtues of Christianity.

These attacks were not confined to the spokesmen of Christian orthodoxy. Representatives of Protestantism contributed their share to it. The father of the Reformation, Martin Luther, began his ministry with a call for improving the status of Jewry, but he was not concerned with enlarging freedom to an underprivileged group. He had the notion that persecutions had solidified Jewish resistance to Christianity, and that an improvement of their lot would make them more receptive to the messages of the church, especially to his new church, which he felt was free of the abuses of the old. Toward Judaism he was always uncompromisingly hostile; and when the Jews did not prove receptive to his call, he turned to bitter hostility toward them. Luther's invective against the Jewish people entered the main stream of German culture to become one of the ingredients of its pronounced anti-Semitism.

The humanists, in many cases, as has been noted previously, looked on the study of Hebrew as part of the classical heritage which they sought to recover. And many Christian divines and men of letters pursued assiduously Hebrew studies, often from Jewish teachers. But this development, too, did not lead directly to a more sympathetic appreciation of Judaism. These students of Hebrew usually sought a knowledge of the Cabbalah, where they believed were secret doctrines confirming some of the truths of Christianity. They were eager to strengthen their own faith, but they were also concerned with using their knowledge as a weapon in their polemics against Judaism.

FROM THE WORLD OF THE CABBALAH

Their enthusiasm for Hebrew studies, as one historian put it, "was not disinterested. Its conscious or subconscious purpose was to confirm or exalt Christianity, to attack Judaism, and, if possible, to convert the Jews." Even Sebastian Muenster whose knowledge of Hebrew literature had earned him the epithet "Rabbi Muenster," waged an active campaign for the conversion of Jews to Christianity.

In a pamphlet called *De Meschia Disputatio* which Muenster published in Basel in 1529 in Hebrew and Latin he presents a disputation between a Jew and a Christian. The introduction well characterizes this work: "In this book," Muenster writes, "the Christian discusses various questions with the brazen Jew concerning the faith of the Jews to show that they are involved in many and grievous errors. For the Lord banished them on account of their sins in refusing to believe in the Messiah who came to this world to redeem from sin everyone who believes in him, and without whom there is no salvation or refuge in heaven and earth. And it is only those who believe in him who constitute a people holy unto the Lord his God, selected by Him to be His own chosen people. But since the Jews refused to accept the belief in our Messiah, they were banished to eternal exile and they are fallen into a darkness of heart to this day."

Another Christian Hebraist, Paulus Fagius, published in 1512 a Latin translation of the missionary pamphlet, *Sefer Emunah* (*A Tractate on Faith*), written by an anonymous apostate from Judaism, to prove that "the beliefs of the followers of Jesus the Messiah who conceive the Holy One blessed be He as father, son, and holy ghost . . . are sound and authentic, and are clearly established on the foundation of the Torah, the prophets and the other writings of sacred Scripture."

These Christian Hebraists generally studied under Jewish teachers, and they had certain sympathies for Jews as individuals, as well as for the values of Jewish culture. Toward Judaism as a living religion, they were, however, all unfriendly.

FROM THE WORLD OF THE CABBALAH

The attacks which emanated from all these sources against Judaism follow a common pattern. They seek to demonstrate by means of text-proofs from Scripture that the Messiah has already come; they argue the superiority of the New Testament over the Old; they assert that Christianity has superseded Judaism, and that Jews who still cling to it, are holding on to an obsolete doctrine; they maintain that the Jews have been rejected by God because of their refusal to embrace the truth offered them, and that the distresses suffered by the Jewish people are a consequence of their guilt in rejecting the Messiahship of Jesus. Above all, they attacked the Talmud as embodying a pernicious morality and as leading those who live by it to falsehood and evil.[1]

CHAPTER 2

THE BATTLE OF SCRIPTURAL TEXTS

RABBI JUDAH'S REPLY to Christianity is scattered in occasional comments throughout his writings. At times he polemicizes directly, analyzing the views of the adversary and offering a formal reply. At other times the polemic interest is in the background, but he expounds his doctrine in a manner which reckons with the position of Christianity. To one subject of controversy, however, he devoted an entire book. It is *Beer ha-Golah*, which deals with the attacks against the Talmud.

One of the popular text-proofs from which Christian apologists sought to demonstrate that the Messiah had come was Gen. 49:10: "The sceptre shall not depart from Judah and a ruler from between his feet until the coming of Shiloh." Shiloh was identified with the Messiah according to the traditional commentaries of both Judaism and Christianity. The text thus appears to assert that a Jewish sovereign authority will end, following the coming of the Messiah. Since the termination of Jewish self-government coincided with the time of Jesus, Scripture thus seems to imply that Jesus was the Messiah. This piece of Biblical exegesis was brought up in the famous disputation of Paul of Burgos against Nahmanides. Rabbi Judah also discusses this on several occasions. His answer is similar to the one given by Nahmanides. The tribe of Judah was promised ascendancy in the leadership of the Jewish people. Scripture asserts that until Messianic times, whenever there will be a sovereign authority in Israel, it will be exercised by a descendant of the tribe of Judah. Following the advent of the Messiah, however, the scepter will cease to be a symbol of sovereignty, for then men will live by ready consent, and there will be no need to coerce them to good citizenship in the community.

Rabbi Judah adds, however, that such promises must not be taken too literally. "I am surprised at those who raise this question," he writes. "Is it necessary that the condition here promised shall prevail forever, in unbroken continuity? Were the judges who held office prior to the establishment of the monarchy in Israel of Judaic origin? Were the Maccabean kings descendants of the tribe of Judah?" Biblical prophecies foreshadow the general direction of events, but they are not a precise blue-print to history. We must not expect that events, as they unfold, correspond in all details to what those prophecies had projected.

Another verse in dispute was Deuteronomy 18:15. After Moses warned his people against consulting "soothsayers" and "diviners" he declared: "A prophet will the Lord thy God raise up unto thee, from the midst of thee, of thy brethren, *like unto me;* unto him shall ye hearken." Some Christian commentators took this as referring to Jesus. *Like unto me* they argued could not possibly refer to Moses, as the obvious meaning of the verse suggests, for Scripture itself (Deu. 34:10) testifies that no prophet ever arose in Israel "like unto Moses." The phrase *like unto me,* they continued to expound, was spoken by God Himself. It prophesied the appearance of a particular prophet of the same status as God, a prophecy which Christians saw fulfilled in Jesus. They then taunted the Jews that their refusal to follow Jesus was a violation of the call: "unto him shall ye hearken."

Rabbi Judah rejected this interpretation indignantly, as a perversion of the text. The term *like* does not posit total equality, but rather similarity in some respects. And it is more plausible to assume that the characterization *like unto me* was spoken by Moses. By accepting the obvious meaning of the text which promises the rise of another prophet like Moses, we imply only that such a prophet would in some respects resemble Moses, not that he would be fully his equal. Moses referred here, Rabbi Judah explained, not to one particular prophet, but to a continuing tradition of prophetic leadership. Moses sought to assure his people that prophets would arise for them in the course of the generations to offer them guidance, even as he offered them guidance. Indeed the force of this characterization is to reject the pretensions of the Christian claim. For only prophets who labored to support the Mosaic law may be said to be like Moses. The Christian church abrogated the Mosaic law.

"Our opponents apply this verse to a particular prophet, and they interpret *like unto me* as meaning that he would be fully his equal, but it would be better for them to remain silent. For it is possible to interpret against their opinion. *Like unto me* means as I teach you Torah and give you instructions concerning the Torah, and exhort you to observe it always. Prophets functioning toward the same ends will the Lord raise unto you, for they will all direct their labors toward strengthening the Mosaic law. . . . As for the one they chose, and his disciples, they and their work are contrary to the law of Moses."[2]

Another common argument for Christianity was the alleged inadequacy of the Hebrew Bible. Thus its assurances of reward or punishment, in consequence of obedience or disobedience to God's will, tend to be stated in material terms. They are formulated in terms of results accruing to man's physical life, or to his society, rather than to the fate of his soul in the hereafter. We therefore need the New Testament where these fulfillments are raised to the level of the spiritual and the other worldly, where the individual soul is made the center in the scheme of salvation. This contrast between the Old and the New Testament was made by John Calvin in his *Institutes*, and it is one of the issues on which the Christian spokesmen challenged Rabbi Hasdai Crescas and Rabbi Joseph Albo in public disputations on the relative merits of Judaism and Christianity.

Rabbi Judah believed in a hereafter and in a law of retribution at work after death. There were, according to Rabbi Judah, rational grounds to support this belief. It was a necessary inference from the belief in divine providence. Since human affairs in this world do not always correspond to the demands of equity, we must assume a longer span of time for that law to function. The belief in a hereafter, Rabbi Judah also reasoned, is a necessary corollary to our doctrine of human dignity. Man's life on this plane of existence is too frail and brief and often sordid in itself to embody the total destiny of one who is God's choicest creation.

There had to be some correlation between cause and effect, according to a popular conviction in medieval culture. Man begins his career on earth from a preceding non-existence, and when his span of years is done he returns to non-existence, which is death. But in what way does he correspond to his divine Maker? Admittedly we cannot seek a full correspondence between a creature and God. On the other hand, "a situation such as this, where there is no correspondence at all between them—this is impossible." Thus we must assume a new level of existence in a hereafter when man sheds his bodily life with all its imperfections. Then will man attain his similarity to the perfect source whence he derives—God.

But Rabbi Judah dissociated himself from the conventional conceptions of the hereafter. He interpreted it all in figurative, and in spiritual terms. The hereafter for him was a state of bodiless existence, and neither its rewards nor its punishments were physical. Its joys were constant union with God. Its misery was the misery of alienation from God, which dooms one to what tradition described by the term "hell"—a state of barrenness, of vanity, and non-existence. But it is not a static barrenness which is represented by hell. It is rather the surrender of life to a fiercely active force, the force of disintegration and death that becomes operative on any being when the good that gives it stability and positive life is withdrawn.

The description of hell with its fiery, lurid tortures, Rabbi Judah interpreted figuratively. Indeed, the hell to which the wicked doom themselves is, according to Rabbi Judah, operative even in this world. "There is no doubt," wrote Rabbi Judah, "that hell, which is the lot of the wicked, extends its power to this world. In many respects the laws of hell are at work in this world.... And these matters are not at all physical, but it is all a mental conception. The whole meaning of hell is deterioration and failure for any living being.... Hell is total non-existence."

Why did the Hebrew Bible say so little about heaven and hell, and about a retribution awaiting man in a hereafter? Rabbi Judah's explanation was that in the nature of things, the belief in the hereafter is not an area of our religion in which we can expect the prophets to instruct us. The prophetic vision, which created the Bible, has its own delimitations; it is not especially competent to speak about the hereafter. For the prophets speak out of that which they experience, and their experience necessarily ends at the frontiers of our own world. They may speak about God, because God is not "removed from this world, for He created it and He continues to guide it." The hereafter, however, is a realm of being entirely outside the range of human experience and the prophetic competence does not extend to what lies beyond man. Here, at least, is one sphere of life where the promptings of reason carry us farther than the intuitions of prophecy. This is one reason for the omission of explicit teaching in the Torah concerning the hereafter.

The Hebrew Bible, moreover, fails to emphasize a personal reward and punishment in the hereafter, Rabbi Judah added, because it sought to avoid pragmatic motivations in religion. One should serve God because of one's love for Him, and one should observe the commandments because they embody God's will. To conform because of expectations of reward or fear of punishment is to be motivated by ulterior considerations. Scripture therefore avoided these, summoning men to seek perfection for its own sake.

It was indeed more important, Rabbi Judah argued, to emphasize the social rather than the purely personal and otherworldly level of retribution. There was no need to assert that by obeying God's law one draws close to Him, and thereby attains a spiritual reward. This was a commonly acknowledged truth. The Hebrew Bible was, however, also concerned with the state of the world. It sought to guide man toward the perfection of the world, toward the removal of the tyrannies and injustices that ravage mankind. And it sought to make it clear that the commandments of the Torah offer men a therapy by which this perfection of the world can be achieved.

The emphasis on other-worldliness, Rabbi Judah finally added, would in fact be a source of weakness rather than of strength to religion, for it would base religion on what cannot be clearly demonstrated or experienced in the only life we know—our life in this world. Thus "we reply to the gentiles who challenge us as to why the Torah does not mention the hereafter. It is certainly proper that the true Torah shall include only what can be ascertained by our experience. That which is a foundation of religion cannot be something which is not discernible to experience. Otherwise anyone might improvise a religion and promise rewards in the hereafter and call on people to believe him. The Torah has therefore avoided mentioning the hereafter deliberately. It is as though it proclaimed thereby that any religion which, like the religion of Moses, offers promises that may be verified by experience is true, unlike other religions which posit notions whose truth has not been authenticated." Rabbi Judah then added a word of criticism at Christianity's claim that its truth is attested to by miracles which were brought by its founders. "We cannot regard this as authentication," he explained, "for it can be contradicted. They say it was . . . thus; others say it was not thus."[3]

The most fundamental cleavage between Christianity and Judaism was over the role of the Jewish people and its Torah in the scheme of man's salvation. Christian theologians agreed that the Hebrew Bible was a divine document, and they recognized it as part of the Holy Scriptures. The Hebrew Bible prescribes a code of law, ceremonial as well as social, by which man was to order his life. Obedience to this law is deemed in the Hebrew Bible as man's way of attaining his highest spiritual ends, of gaining his salvation. Christian doctrine challenged this, declaring that the law as a way of salvation had been operative only before the coming of Jesus, but that henceforth salvation was to be by faith, faith especially in the messiahship of Jesus.

This doctrine of Christianity was occasionally supported by certain conceptions in Jewish thought. The Talmud, for instance, teaches: "There will be an abrogation of commandments in the hereafter." The hereafter stands for an epoch when men will have attained perfection in response to the recognition of God's universal power, righteousness, and love. The teachers who propounded this conception, it was argued, must have believed that when human character will have attained a high degree of moral refinement, there will be no need of external direction for man's behaviour. Men will then do the right thing automatically, in a spontaneous outpouring of love for God and for his fellow-creatures. Since Christians assumed that Jesus was the Messiah, they reasoned that the stage of human perfection had already come. Thus law was no longer a necessity, for it had been replaced with a new way to God, the way of the Messiah, which they equated with the way of Jesus.

It was not only the ceremonial law, and not only the Jewish law as such which came under challenge. All law became suspect, being looked upon as something coercive, external, unspiritual. This revolt against law was expounded particularly by the apostle Paul, but it entered the mainstream of Christian thought. The full scope of Paul's revolt against the law is well characterized by George Foote Moore: "The peculiarity of Paul's anti-nomianism is the substitution of enthusiasm in the literal sense, for the law of nature reflected in the individual and common conscience, as well as for the law in Scripture and tradition; and it was precisely in the moral field that this theory had the most radical consequences" (*Judaism,* Cambridge 1927, II p.10).

The spokesmen of Christianity granted that the Jews had once enjoyed a high mission in life. They had been made the custodians of divine revelation. But having refused to follow the path of revelation to its highest summons, having refused to acknowledge Jesus as the Messiah, the Christian argument continued, the Jews had forfeited that high station. Christian theology allowed itself to speak of the Jews as having been rejected by God, rejected because of their stubbornness in refusing the new dispensation. In still clinging to a religion centered in law, it was argued, the Jews were a fossil of a once great people, which had doomed itself to spiritual sterility by holding on to an obsolete institution.

The Christian exposition of this doctrine was for the most part dogmatic. It flowed from an assumption, which could not be proven. It rested on an act of faith, the one act of faith which made one a Christian. There were on the other hand certain auxiliary arguments occasionally cited against the Jewish belief in the continuing authority of the law. Thus it was argued that salvation could not possibly depend on the law. For Biblical law is so extensive and manifold, and how could one person ever hope to fulfill all its demands? Indeed, were not some elements in that law beyond realization altogether? The entire cult of Temple sacrifices which looms so large in Biblical law had become a dead letter as a result of the destruction of the Temple in Jerusalem. A God of mercy and love could not possibly link man's chances for salvation with demanding what in the nature of things was beyond man's performance. The empirical facts of Jewish suffering in the diaspora, too, were used to prove that the Jews must obviously have been abandoned by God, or else He would not allow His chosen ones to be treated so shabbily at the hands of men.

Rabbi Judah examined all these elements in the thesis of Christianity, and he retorted accordingly. He argued that the

FROM THE WORLD OF THE CABBALAH

Christian position was in part built on a confusion between the phenomenon of law as a social institution and particular laws which are directed at specific goals in a given time. Laws change and disappear, but law as an institution persists despite the change. The Talmudic doctrine about the abrogation of commandments referred to individual, particular laws. Obviously a moral transformation on so far-reaching a scale as would be represented in the dawn of the Messianic age would spell vast changes in all social institutions. Among those changes will undoubtedly be the obsolescence of certain laws, directed at ends which will by then have been fully realized. Even in that plane of existence, however, some laws will still be necessary, some channels through which life was to find its direction. Thus the Talmud declared explicitly that Purim, the typical story of the perils the Jewish people endured, and their miraculous deliverance, as well as the Day of Atonement which occasions man's quest for spiritual renewal, would remain operative even in the Messianic age. For while some laws were intended to serve no more than temporary ends, others have a permanent character. Particular laws, temporary in their purpose, will be abrogated, but the law as an institution will remain in force.

Rabbi Judah dealt with the argument that the multiplicity of Biblical laws doomed man to forfeit salvation for no one person could possibly fulfill them all. Here we have, of course, he pointed out, a misunderstanding as to the goal of the law. In its entirety it is addressed not to the individual but to the community. The individual is expected to carry out such laws which come within the scope of his own life. A man is judged not by the quantity of laws observed, but by the general direction of his life. He has met his responsibility if his conduct reveals a preponderance of good over evil, a preponderance of actions which conform to God's will rather than those which deviate from it. The law is a source of directives available to guide man in his life, to the extent that situations arise to which such directives may apply. There was never any intention on the part of the divine law giver, however, that any one man attempt to carry out all enactments in the law code.[4]

Rabbi Judah carried his analysis to the more fundamental question: Can we assume a sudden break in God's plan for man's salvation, a revolutionary abrogation of one Testament and its replacement with a new one? Can we assume God's selection of a people for a high mission, and then its rejection? His conception of God did not permit him to believe so.

The drama of divine revelation was not a casual process, contingent upon man's initiative. It was, according to the common conviction of Judaism as well as Christianity, an eruption into history of God's own initiative. It was an injection into history of a divine plan for the perfection of all life. The Hebrew Bible was the record of this process. The Biblical law was the crystallization of its imperatives. Israel was its custodian, its protagonist, chosen to administer as well as to disseminate it. All this suggests not a temporary episode, but a permanent design, to endure as long as man's adventure on earth endures.

The Christian argument was of course that Israel's sin in rejecting Jesus had released a new condition in history, and that this new condition had destroyed Israel's convenant with God. But can a father-son relationship be severed because a child misbehaves? The relationship between God and Israel was not a contingent relationship, created because Israel had met certain prior conditions. It was ultimately a relationship created in an act of God's own free choice. It thus became part of the scheme of things flowing from the pattern of creation. Only one analogy exists for that kind of relationship, and that is the bond that ties father to son, a permanent bond, in other words. "The Lord chose Israel not because of their righteousness and their worthy deeds, but His was an unconditional choice . . . and therefore we cannot say that as the cause is removed (the righteousness of Israel), the consequence—their selection as His people—will be removed also. It is true that their conduct, for good or for evil, resulted in making them closer to

God or more distant from Him. . . . The essence of the election, however, did not hinge on any action on their part at all."

It is unthinkable Rabbi Judah argued, that God has selected another people to be the people of Torah. A culture expresses a people's distinctiveness. Israel's relationship to the Torah was not arbitrary. The Torah is organically related to Israel's unique gifts as a people. No other people can arbitrarily step into their place, for no other people has those characteristics. "Every existent being has its own pattern which is distinctive to itself, and this pattern is not suitable for anyone else. The pattern of the Torah and the commandments is adapted only to Israel; the Torah is their pattern, distinctive to themselves, and it cannot be for any other people, as you may judge for yourself. Although they profess loyalty to the Torah, they have not penetrated to its depths, in order to observe it. . . . Thus it has been made clear that the election of Israel is a necessary element in the order of existence, a derivation from the necessity of the Torah, which is indispensable for the world, and which cannot be without Israel. . . . And how can we conceive of the elimination and the voiding of something that is necessary?"

Rabbi Judah conceded readily that there may be temporary alienations between Israel and God. Their authentic nature, however, remains unchanged even then. The selection to their high role in history consisted essentially in a particular endowment. All men are of course capable of responding to God; they are all made in His image. But in Israel this gift is present in its greatest bounty. The Creator who formed them and assigned to them their destiny poured into their beings those unique gifts of character, those specialized capacities, which are particularly essential for the cultivation of divine pursuits. One may temporarily be alienated from his calling and neglect to make the most of his capacities, but the capacities remain. And once a person becomes again reconciled to his destiny, the capacities are there as the ready tools with which he is again to do his work. "The capacity with which

FROM THE WORLD OF THE CABBALAH

Israel was endowed to play its high role did not disappear, as a person who acquired intelligence, and then turned to dissipation and forgot all his learning, did not lose permanently his capacities to acquire wisdom, and he remains equipped to acquire it, whenever he should return to his course."

There are no abrogations in the basic fabric of nature, Rabbi Judah continued, and we cannot concede any abrogations in the divine plan. The endowments of a people are never voided. Nor can a people that is without such endowments, replace them and take over their function. "It cannot be that those who are without the necessary capacities shall become the recipients of these divine matters, or that those who are endowed with these capacities shall have their capacities voided." Even miracles only alter the properties in things temporarily, but permanent modifications of any element in the plan by which God directs the universe are inconceivable.[5]

Rabbi Judah also examined the claim that the facts of Jewish suffering in the diaspora tended to suggest that God must have abandoned Israel, or else He would surely have stepped in to protect them. As Rabbi Judah saw it, the remarkable fact about Israel's fate in the diaspora is not that they were persecuted, but that they survived despite their persecutions. Considering all the conspiracies which evil men launched repeatedly to exterminate them, the miracle is that they remained alive. Indeed, Israel's survival must be seen as a mark of God's protection and love.

Suffering, moreover, Rabbi Judah continued with pathos, is not always an indication of sin. The ascription of sin to the sufferer is often a glib generalization that does violence to the cause of a noble man. In an evil world, suffering is very often the lot of a noble man, and his distress is then a badge of distinction. The sufferings of the Jewish people are not a reflection of its own failures, but of the failures of mankind. The unpopularity of the Jews stemmed from the very mission to which they were summoned; and it was incidental to it. For the world in its immaturity, its lack of enlightenment sensed a profound antagonism between its way, and the way of the Torah, with its call for a radical transformation of its culture and life. And it transferred its antagonism to those who stand as the witnesses of the Torah. The Jews were disliked because they were a moral irritant in mankind. That dislike was the price the Jews were called on to pay for their vocation as aids in the drama of man's redemption.

Rabbi Judah did not claim that the Jews lived in history without blemish. On the contrary he was conscious and profoundly so, of their many shortcomings. These shortcomings were in part the consequences of the conditions under which they lived. The persecutions visited upon them often produced a moral deterioration in Jewry. It led them occasionally to moral cynicism, and to a loss of faith in divine providence. But there were more fundamental reasons for those lapses. Their very position as the people of the Torah exposed them to special possibilities of failure. With every special talent there always go new sources of peril. For the possession of a talent is no ready guarantee as to how it will be used, man remaining a free agent. And the very unique gifts with which the Lord endowed the Jews created the possibility that these gifts might be misused. The greater the man, moreover, the greater his temptations. For life appears to abhor deviations from the commonplace, and all kinds of hostile forces arise to tempt and to assail the strange challenger. The behavior of Jews at any given time cannot, therefore, be in every instance a performance of unmitigated moral perfection.

There is finally the fact that not all men are to be judged by the same standard. Lapses of conduct count more heavily against the Jews because they live under a higher charge. As the people of the Torah, they stand under more exacting commitments. As a sensitive Jew, he felt very humble about the moral condition within his own Jewish community. Much too often there was quite a gap between performance and expectation.

Yes, Rabbi Judah conceded, there is one sense in which the sufferings of the Jewish people may be regarded as a consequence of their own guilt. The failure of mankind is in a measure an indication that the Jews have not yet performed their task in the world. They have not yet converted the world toward God. Though Israel's mission began with the patriarch Abraham, large elements of mankind have remained in darkness. These unredeemed elements of mankind which remained outside "the wings of the Shekinah" (the divine Presence) have been the source of all the antagonism visited upon Israel in exile.

If we wish to look upon this failure to complete their mission as a sin, then we may say that Israel's sufferings are the result of sin. Israel cannot, however, be held entirely culpable for the failure of its mission, Rabbi Judah continued to explain. For this kind of a failure, this kind of sin, is in a sense inevitable in the early stages of civilization. The conversion of mankind and its total redemption is a slow process. And the very people who are responsible for serving as its protagonists in history require a growing comprehension of their task, and a growing maturity in performing it.

The sufferings endured by the Jewish people in the world, Rabbi Judah was confident, play a positive role in bringing them ever closer to a consciousness of their task. For sufferings tend to purge them of their own imperfection, and to stir them toward a deeper awareness of the stakes involved in the service of their cause. Israel's failures and sufferings are thus incidents in the drama of progress by which life is moving on toward ever greater perfection.

As Rabbi Judah saw the facts, Israel's destiny appeared to be intertwined with the destiny of all mankind. And the very circumstances which had doomed the Jewish people to be in the world, but not altogether of it, had also assured them of the promise of survival. For Israel's life, its triumphs, its defeats, as well as its sufferings, were all incidents in the performance of a mission, which was indispensable to the world's salvation. Man was launched in the world as a free, unfinished being, who was to grow toward his own perfection. And he was to attain this through the workings of a leavening process which had been made part of the very texture of history. That leavening process was to proceed through the gradual impregnation of life with the moral and spiritual teachings as embodied in the Hebrew Bible, of which the Jewish people remained as the custodians and protagonists. If Israel were to disappear, one of the indispensable conditions for the furtherance of God's plan in history would disappear also. This is inconceivable. As Rabbi Judah put it: "Israel is the essence and foundation of the world. Indeed, Israel may be considered as contributing the element of form to the world's otherwise chaotic and undisciplined character. And if Israel should, God forbid, perish, the whole world would fail."[6]

CHAPTER 3

THE MESSIANIC HOPE
AND THE DOCTRINE OF TIME

THE BRIDGE THAT LINKED the gap between Israel's suffering and the faith in future vindication was the doctrine of the Messiah. On the day of Messianic realization, when the good latent in man will be made manifest, and a world order of justice and peace will be established for mankind, then will Israel's period of distress come to an end. But when will this great day arise? How long will the era of travail and suffering continue? Rabbi Judah explored these questions in all their ramifications, in order to guide his people in meeting the most crucial issue which challenged them.

Rabbi Judah opposed the tendency among some Cabbalists to conjecture the date of the Messiah's arrival. Through the ingenious interpretation of Biblical verses, in which letters were transposed with their numerical equivalents, various hints were found in the Bible as to the precise time of the redemption. This tendency became especially pronounced after the expulsion from Spain in 1492. These Messianic speculations offered assurances for the moment, but they opened the door to catastrophic disillusionment, as the promises on which men pinned their hopes were frustrated. Rabbi Judah warned against all this, as a perilous venture. We cannot lift the veil which covers the unknown, no matter how deeply the heart yearns to know the reassuring word. But Rabbi Judah summoned his people to hold on to their faith that in the fullness of time the long awaited redemption would surely come.

Rabbi Judah's assurances of ultimate redemption did not stem merely from the prophecies of Scripture. They were rooted in his understanding of the universe, and in his conception of the processes of history. Rabbi Judah applied to the problem of the Jewish people the medieval conception of a "natural place." It derived ultimately from Aristotle, but it was one of the basic conceptions in all medieval interpretations of the world. Even Copernicus employed it. This conception asserted that every object in existence has a place which is natural to itself. Temporarily it may be jolted from this place, but eventually it must resume its natural position, or else it will totally disintegrate.

Every nation, explained Rabbi Judah has its natural place, a territory proper to itself. Israel's natural place is Palestine. The dispersion of Israel, which removed them from their natural place is therefore contrary to nature. It has produced a deterioration in the land. It has made the land barren and desolate; and even its dimensions seem to have shrunken. For only Israel can evoke from that land its best. It is only when Israel inhabits it that that "land flourishes and then it reveals its inner excellence in all things."

Exile has, however, produced its most serious deterioration in Israel itself. A people in exile is a contradiction of the laws of nature. A people cannot persist thus, except for a limited time. Then, if the people is not to disintegrate, there must be a return. "The dispersion itself is evidence and clear proof of eventual redemption, for the dispersion is clearly a change, a deviation from the order of nature. The Lord, blessed be He, provided for every nation to reside in its proper place, and He provided for Israel a place proper to them, and this is *Eretz Yisrael*. For them to be exiled from their place is a radical change and deviation. And all things that leave their natural place and find themselves outside their place cannot subsist . . . but they return to their natural place. . . The nature with which God endowed each being gives it durability so that it persists permanently, and if what is unnatural were also to endure permanently although it is not in accordance with the order and nature of existence, then the nature of that being would become something vain and superfluous, without need. This cannot be."

A derivative of the conception of the "natural place" was the doctrine that parts of any organic whole tend to reunite. "The dispersion is similarly unnatural, and as each being tends to return to its place, so the parts which are scattered and separated reassemble to become one whole." The application of this principle to the Jewish people was obvious. The dispersion of Israel among the nations is contrary to nature. "As they are one people it is proper that they be together and united, like all beings in nature which are not divided in two, but gather to be one. . . . If this dispersion were to last indefinitely, then, what is unnatural would become natural."

Rabbi Judah's principle led him to affirm national freedom as a demand of nature, against which every form of national domination must eventually prove ineffectual. "According to the order of nature it is not proper that one nation be subservient to another . . . for the Lord, blessed be He, intended each nation to be independent. . . . And if exile were to endure permanently and nations always exercise their might over Israel, then this condition would be contrary to the order of existence. . . . Such a thing cannot be. And thus from the facts of exile we may draw inferences which point to the redemption."

The deviation from nature does not of course always return to conform to nature. It faces another alternative—to disintegrate and perish. But as Rabbi Judah beheld the Jewish people he saw ample evidence of vitality and continuing life. The disintegrating tendencies of the dispersion are greatly cancelled out because of certain qualities of Jewish life. These are the study of Torah, the separatism of the Jewish group through a distinctive way of life, particularly diet, the continued consciousness of being in want of restoration. Thus there is engendered a sense of unity among Jews. This sense of unity will enable the Jewish people to triumph over forces of disintegration and death. The logic of the Jewish situation therefore pointed not to disappearance but to rebirth. They will return to a condition of freedom and unity—in the place which is natural to their distinctive characteristics as a people. "There remains the power of unity among the Jews, in the face of exile, and they are not entirely divided. And thanks to this power of unity which survives among them they will yet be gathered together into full unity. . . . Through this power of unity Israel will yet return from exile."

Rabbi Judah was aware that his interpretation made Jewish survival, at least to some extent, contingent upon the behaviour of the Jews themselves. He, therefore, pleaded with them to guard zealously each of these attributes of their group life which contribute to making them a distinct community and which will aid toward their eventual restoration. The most significant source of Jewish separatism is of course religion, the Torah. "The Jews are Jews by virtue of their religion; and without their religion they would cease to be Jews." But even a religious group requires social ties to preserve its identity. Rabbi Judah pleaded for the maintenance of the distinctive Jewish dress. He fought against the use of non-Jewish wine. He denounced the tendency of some Jews to ignore their own courts, and to take their litigations to the civil courts of the state. He was especially emphatic in his plea for Jewish unity. The quarrelsomeness among Jews and their leaders, their tendency to break up into fragmentary entities, to form parties and factions—all magnify the dispersion. On the other hand, their unity is a negation of the dispersion, and will finally permit events to move to their natural climax and restore them to their homeland.[7]

But why is the redemption so slow in coming? Why this long duration of suffering and of waiting? People of his generation asked these questions earnestly. They needed an answer that would make their lot at least, to some extent, intelligible— and thus bearable. Rabbi Judah grappled with these questions. The key to his answer lies in his doctrine of time.

Rabbi Judah followed a conventional, Aristotelian definition of time. As an objective fact, time is the span of solar revolutions. Time has, however, an inner quality. It is also the span of the life process in its movement toward self-realization. God, according to Rabbi Judah, did not enact creation as a finished enterprise. He provided that it evolve toward its full realization in time. Every element in creation, at the time it came into being, was corrupted with deficiency so that it might have scope far growing toward its perfection in a process of progressive development. "The universe which emanated from God is limited at the start, but it proceeds to extend itself. . . . The universe was created by God as a spring which continues to flow and to expand." Life must thus be a process of constant becoming, and time is the key to the mystery as to what is and what will be. "Time brings into realization whatever is to be realized in all beings in the world, for everything depends on time. And because they depend on time, each one finds its realization in its own distinctive time. . . . All things come into being in their own special time."

The movement of events in time, according to Rabbi Judah, is, however, a dual process. It involves destruction no less than creation. Indeed, destruction is a concomitant of creation. Rabbi Judah introduced here the neo-Platonic doctrine of creation through the power of opposites. In ibn Gabirol's *Fons Vitae* it is stated thus: "Since every event is engendered by its opposite, it is also necessary that being shall come from non-being, or what is, from nothingness." It is the element of deficiency, which is an area of non-existence, in any being, that permits its being superseded by other and more perfect forms.

Suffering, privation, destruction take on a positive significance in the light of this doctrine. It is the wreckage of an old life form, which must make room for the new that is struggling to replace it. Rabbi Judah compared it to the breaking of the egg, which enables the chick to enter upon the world, or to the discarding of the shell, when the fruit within has ripened. He saw a symbolic representation of this doctrine in the Scriptural statement that *tohu* and *bohu,* void and nothingness, preceded creation. "In the measure of non-existence, do new existencies come into being. And Scripture intimated this in the creation of the world. Prior to the creation of light, which is the most perfect act of creation, it says that the world was void and without form. Prior to this event there was darkness, which is non-being, for it is impossible for any being to come into existence, except after non-existence."

These principles govern not only individual events in nature. They apply as well to the enterprise of human life as a whole. All of it is within the same grip of time, and subject to its laws. Life considered as a totality is a process of becoming, a movement toward perfection, a quest for self-realization. Toward the end, when the time of the Messiah will arrive, this world will become divine, and men will not be immersed in material, but in divine pursuits. Toward the end the world will also become truly one. For the essential excellence in what is perfect is its unity. . . . "And the essential function of the Messiah will consist in the fact that he is a being who will unite all and perfect all so that this will be truly one world." Incidental to this process is destruction and breakdown, war and social disorganization—the full sweep of suffering and sorrow, from the fall of the Temple in Jerusalem to the contemporary tragedies of Israel in exile; and all the sufferings of mankind itself as well. But while these appear to us as evil when judged out of their context in history, they are as a matter of fact part of the process of new creation. They are all preparatory to the great consummation which lies beyond them. They are the steps by which creation continues to purge itself of its initial deficiencies, the injustices and wrongs that warp human life, and obscure God's universal presence in the world.

But the ground in which all this movement must take place is time. It will come through a flowering, a maturing of forces now acting in life, not through an arbitrary, a catastrophic or miraculous transformation interrupting the flow of history. It will be a movement passing through distinct stages. Moving from total barrenness and primitivism, it enters upon the next stage, the stage of Torah, when the leaven of vital transformation is already at work in the world. And then comes the stage of fulfillment, the time of the Messiah; but even this stage involves a span of time, before the new world will fully come into its own.

The Messiah has not yet appeared, because the world has not yet achieved its fullest self-realization, because we have not as yet reached the climax of history. "The time which is distinctive for the coming of the Messiah, who will unify all, is at the end of days, which is the fulfillment of history. Therefore it ought not to be so baffling to us that the Messiah is so long delayed, for the proper time of his arrival is at the end of time. . . ."

Rabbi Judah was careful to indicate that events, in his view, do not move with automatic inevitability, simply because time moves on. Man has a creative part in the shaping of his and the world's destiny. Human conduct can speed or retard the hour of Messianic realization. However, human conduct cannot affect it in an ultimate sense. For life moves to the design of the Creator, and the end of days is that for which the first days came into being. Regardless of circumstances, the great sought for hour will come, for God's design cannot be thwarted. And thus Rabbi Judah summoned his people to wait with hope, to live with faith. The day of their vindication was bound to arrive.[8]

Chapter 4

IN DEFENSE OF THE TALMUD

RABBI JUDAH'S DEFENSE of the Talmud is a masterpiece of exposition. It analyzes every charge that was part of the general calumny against the Talmud. Patiently he states the problem; patiently he replies to each question. To achieve readability he permits himself occasionally to versify, especially the prefatory remarks to each chapter. At least once he introduces into the text his own name, in acrostic. What emerges is not only a powerful document of polemics, but an excellent study of the Oral Law and its place in Jewish tradition.

The name of the book *Beer ha-Golah,* the Well of Exile, suggests his conception of the Talmud. It is a well of living waters of faith, available to nourish all who thirst for the truth. And each chapter is given the same name, *Beer* or a Well. His own task of defending the Talmud, Rabbi Judah likened to Jacob's feat of lifting the stone from the well when he met Rachel (Gen. 29:1-11). Thus he would cause "its waters to rise higher and higher. . . . Every man of understanding will draw from it. . . . And may its springs spread their abundance over large areas."[9]

The charges against the Talmud which Rabbi Judah considered are representative of the entire field of calumny against Talmudic literature, and many of them are still repeated by foes of Judaism. For those who have sought to disparage Judaism have always directed their invective against this literature which is Judaism's principal source of doctrine, morality, and law. The first charge which was levelled against the Talmud was that it was an unwarranted appendage to the Bible, that the Talmudists had changed Biblical laws, adding to them and subtracting from them, thereby violating the authority of Scripture.

Rabbi Judah denounced the notion that the Bible was a finished and final work and that it intended to freeze our religious life, and to halt the flow of new religious creativity. What would be objectionable would be to take a Biblical law which has specific provisions and changing it arbitrarily, as adding a day to the prescribed number of days in a particular festival. What the rabbis did was nothing of the sort. They made the Bible a living power in the world by making of it a flexible doctrine, that had within itself the power of new development.

Rabbi Judah surveyed each type of Biblical supplementation, which appears in the Talmud. There is the element of interpretation. Many Biblical statements are ambiguous. Details indispensable for the proper execution of its laws are omitted. The Talmudists in removing ambiguities, in clearing up passages of uncertain meaning, are surely not "changing" the Bible. What they have to offer is implicit in the Bible, and is really a part of it.

There are enactments of the rabbis, which are clearly of their own deliberation and decision, but they are linked with the Bible through the so-called *asmakhta,* or derivative support. Rabbi Judah analyzed the typical cases of *asmakhta* and showed that the support is genuine, that, in every instance, an authentic implication of Scripture was drawn upon and then employed as a link between the old and the new. Those enactments were never given the authority of Scriptural law. They had the status of rabbinic enactments. But they surely are not inconsistent with Scripture.

Another category of Talmudic supplementation is the precautionary statute, designed to safeguard Biblical law. Thus the rabbis ordained that the evening recitations of the *Shema* which proclaims God's unity, prescribed in the Bible for the time "when thou liest down" was to take place before the evening meal. No such requirement appears in the Bible itself. But the rabbinic injunction was inspired by the fear that a person would continue to defer his obligation, and then, affected by drowsiness he would retire, without reciting the *Shema* at all.

The rabbinic injunction here added to what is prescribed in the Bible, but only as a safeguard, to assure the proper observance of Biblical law. Such enactments clearly harmonize with the Bible. As in nature, the more vital organs are provided with other organs to guard them against injury—the eye has the eyelid, the hands and feet have nails to protect the fingers. So is it in order for the rabbis utilizing the intelligence which the Lord has given them to create a body of safeguards, which will keep people from transgressing the fundamentals of Biblical law.

There is a body of Talmudic law, which it is true, represents independent enactments of the rabbis, as the institution of the commemoration of Hanukkah. However, there is here also perfect congruity with Scripture. As in nature, there is continuous creation, supplementing the initial process by which the universe came into being, so in Torah, there must be continuous creation. The fundamentals are stated in Scripture. But the rabbis were inspired with the wisdom to supplement them with new provisions in accordance with their judgement, as needs arose. But they are all part of one process, the quest to perfect life.[10]

Another charge was that Talmudic law is often contrary to reason. Thus the Talmud ruled that no verdict of guilty shall be valid in criminal cases, where capital punishment was involved, unless at least one member in the panel of juror-judges shall have spoken in favor of the defendant. A unanimous verdict against the defendant was not to be sustained. This, it was argued, is against all common sense. Rabbi Judah defended the opinion of the Talmud on the ground that it was an important precaution against a miscarriage of justice. Every person, even the worst offender, has some extenuating circumstances in his favor. It is only when he has protagonists among the juror-judges that we can be sure that the evidence has been thoroughly sifted, and that the defendant has been given the benefit of every doubt. Otherwise what may dominate the scene is the passion of prejudice, or a superficial examination of the facts, without reckoning with all the complexities which underlie the actions of men.

There were various other criticisms. In some passage the Talmudists were accused of misinterpreting the Biblical text. Especially the folk poetry of the *agadah* came under attack as constituting a body of fanciful and clearly impossible tales. In these tales, too, God is often described in grossly anthropomorphic terms, as though He were a magnified human being, sharing in all those feelings and actions which characterize the careers of mortal men.

Rabbi Judah analyzed the specific passages cited in the indictment. Invariably he demonstrates that the critics read their text with carelessness and superficiality. The so-called "absurd" actions ascribed by the Talmudists to God, for instance, Rabbi Judah explained as poetic and figurative expressions which are only intended to give vividness to the statements about God's work in the universe. The Talmud only followed the style of the Bible, which similarly permits itself to speak of God in corporeal terms, and for the same reason.

The rabbis, moreover, Rabbi Judah continued, lived centuries ago and they employed forms of expression peculiar to their own time. We may find those expressions baffling, but once we overcome the strangeness of an unfamiliar idiom, we shall find them all conveying a valid and a precious truth. In any case "shall we speak ill of them because we cannot comprehend their words? Indeed, it should not surprise us if we cannot grasp the inward meaning of their words. The great distance which separates our time from theirs also separates our wisdom from theirs. . . . The difference in time makes for differences between their wisdom and ours. . . ."[11]

Rabbi Judah then considered the accusation that Talmudic discussions reveal ignorance of the sciences. Thus the rabbis ascribe everything to divine providence and ignore what the scientists regard as the natural causes of things. However, explained Rabbi Judah, "the rabbis did not deal with the natural cause at all. . . . That is the domain of natural scientists or physicians, not of the rabbis. They only talked of the cause which determines nature itself, and anyone who rejects this denies all religion and the Torah. . . . For all things have a natural cause which determines it. But transcending that natural cause there is a divine cause, which is the cause of that cause. And this is what the rabbis talked of."[12]

The final criticism considered by Rabbi Judah was the charge that Talmud teaches a parochial morality, that it disparages the *am ha-aretz* (literally "the people of the land"), who was identified with the ignorant man, that it shows contempt for non-Jews, and that it contains references which are offensive toward Christianity. Rabbi Judah denied that the Talmudic disparagements of the *am ha-aretz* are an injustice toward the uneducated masses of people. As Rabbi Judah interpreted it, the *am ha-aretz* is not primarily an ignorant person. One who lacks knowledge and attempts to correct his shortcomings by seeking guidance from those above him, is holding his proper place in the hierarchy of life; he is beyond criticism.

The *am ha-aretz* criticised in the Talmud, Rabbi Judah explained, is the person who is aware of his ignorance but is indifferent to his plight. He does not try to improve himself by becoming a disciple of some master who can guide and inspire him. He thus withdraws himself from the hierarchy of relations which can lift his life from what it is and direct it toward God. As every bodily organ must draw its sustenance from the heart, so must every person, regardless of his intellectual status at any time, place himself in active relation to some source of Torah. The study of Torah is the greatest privilege as well as the greatest responsibility of any man; it must be discharged by each in accordance with his capacities, and in accordance with the state of his intellectual development. When he neglects that, he has brought reproach upon his own head. As far as the dignity of human beings is concerned, the rabbis "did not depreciate the value of human beings at all, but everything depends on their works."

Rabbi Judah similarly denied any hostility in Judaism toward people of another faith. All passages cited for such criticism deal, according to Rabbi Judah, with idolators. They have no reference to those who practice the so-called seven Noahite laws, these elements of a universal religious and moral code, which, from the standpoint of Judaism, qualifies a man for the highest worth in the sight of God, regardless of the particular religion he may profess. Toward such people Judaism ordains the highest respect and solicitude. Indeed, such men really form one fellowship with Israel. The one universal God they revere in common "links them and forges them into a unity."

The prayer in the Amidah which imprecates against the enemies of Israel—the so-called *Birkat ha-Minim,* is similarly not an expression of hostility toward other people, as a social group. The enemies of Israel here referred to are those who either seek to undermine Israel's religion through the propagation of contrary beliefs or those who seek to deny Israel the liberty to pursue its own life. It refers to the dictators who have always seen in Judaism a system of life antagonistic to their own, because Judaism centers human loyalty on the absolute, on one universal God, and thus nullifies the claims to absolute loyalty which are made by and in behalf of men.

These prayers, moreover, are not directed against erring individuals. They are directed against error itself. And what they look forward to is that truth shall vanquish falsehood. They pray that evil men shall be no more, because they shall have gone through an inner purification, because they shall have been transformed through repentance, and join the fellowship of the good.

As to the charge that the Talmud is guilty of statements opposed to Christianity, Rabbi Judah also felt that there had been much misunderstanding, much misinterpretation of fact. As a rule, the rabbis did not indulge in disparaging remarks about other religions. They pursued a positive program. They sought to expound their own faith; and "one cannot speak excessively thereon." There may be some passages which lend themselves to objectionable interpretation, but the great commentators of the Talmud have clarified those statements, and whoever wants the correct interpretation can find it; and much of what is now regarded as offensive will then be no more.

Assuming, however, that the Talmudists expressed themselves against Christianity, why, asked Rabbi Judah, should there be so much agitation against them? One should welcome criticism and the contrary views of opponents "because of a love for research and for knowledge, especially since they did not intend primarily to stir up controversy, but to expound their own faith. . . . One ought not to reject the words of an opponent. It is preferable to seek them out and study them. . . . Thus shall a person arrive at the . . . full truth." "Suppose then," Rabbi Judah continued, "that they actually did so speak against Christian doctrines, and expressed in public what was in their heart. Is this an evil thing? Not at all. One can reply to them. . . . The conclusion of the matter is that it would be most unworthy to suppress books in order to silence teachers like them."[13]

VI

The Legacy of Rabbi Judah

THE LEGACY OF RABBI JUDAH

IN THE HISTORY OF CULTURE the pendulum has often oscillated between rationalism and mysticism. Each has a contribution to make toward the human quest for meaning in this bewildering world, which is our home. When mysticism dominates the scene, we need the cool probing of reason to prevent an uncritical surrender to obscurantism. But when reason has proclaimed her sovereignty then reason needs to be reminded of her limitations. The sixteenth century was an age when mysticism was in flower, as the esoteric literature of the Cabbalah continued to fascinate ever larger circles in European society. Rabbi Judah was one of the most vivid and colorful figures of that new age, of its hopes and achievements.

Rabbi Judah helped emancipate Jewish thought from the constraining discipline of scholasticism. In its own time scholasticism was a positive achievement. It brought religion into harmony with science, and it made an impressive gesture toward assigning a significant role for reason in life. But in the course of the centuries scholasticism exposed its deficiency. With all the subtlety of Maimonides, who had drawn the blueprints of that harmonization, the scholastic episode in religious thought was based on a basically defective hypothesis. In its attempt to fashion all culture into a comprehensive unity, it made religion the peak of a pyramid. The foundation of that pyramid was to be natural science. Through a knowledge of nature, one was to move to an awareness of the God Who was the source of its being. Religion was thus enmeshed in the limitations of any science which may be prevalent at a particular period of time.

Scholasticism took Aristotle as the unerring authority in natural science. As knowledge grew and life advanced, it became apparent, however, that Aristotle was not an infallible guide to truth. Many of his conceptions proved false and unreliable. The difficulty to which this failure pointed was fundamental. It was not merely that the science of Aristotle was defective. It is in the nature of all knowledge attained by mortal minds that it embodies only a relative truth, and that the "truths" of today become the mythologies of tomorrow. The fusion of religion with any particular doctrine in science thus imposes upon it the limitations of a relative truth. It gives it a measure of timeliness, of "relevance" for the people of a given age, but it tends to compromise its truth for those who follow, when the winds of doctrine have changed, and new theories dominate the minds of thinking men.

The rigidity of scholastic thought, moreover, had alienated men from reality. Abstract universals were superimposed upon concrete facts, as men sought truth through syllogistic reasoning rather than through contact with reality. The "science" which flourished under scholasticism was similarly based on speculation and logical analysis, invariably employing some Aristotelian text as the highest authority to lean on. But syllogisms and logical demonstrations cannot take the place of the observation of nature. It was through emancipation from the theoretic spinning of abstract concepts, that the real world could come into full view, to be read with fresh objectivity. The fruit of this reaction was the inauguration of modern science. It has sometimes been assumed that the rise of modern science was a phase of the triumphant march of reason. But as Whitehead has pointed out, the scientific movement was "the return to the contemplation of brute fact; and it was based in the recoil from the inflexible rationality of medieval thought."[1]

Rabbi Judah agreed with the mystics that it is possible to attain closeness to God in an act of direct experience. For is it really necessary to know all the intricacies of the phenomena in nature before attaining the mood of awe for the divine source of existence? Is it necessary to know the chemistry of a flower before testifying that it is beautiful? Must we resolve all the baffling questions as to the unfolding of a child's life before we can feel the wonder of the process which is at work in it? The scholastics had yielded too much ground to Aristotle. They had exaggerated the role of reason in life. Men can know with the heart and not only with the mind. They can know directly, in moments of intimate experience, of intuitive grasp and illumination, without the ponderous operations of syllogistic reasoning.

We can recognize the wonder of life and feel an awed reverence for God, even though we have not subjected the facts of existence to meticulous analysis in order to see the precise steps by which they have their being. Rabbi Judah proclaimed this liberating doctrine. Knowledge, including a knowledge of the sciences, may help us in our quest for God, but we are not dependent on it. Religion is an autonomous expression of the human spirit. And sensitive spirits can experience the love of God in a direct out-reaching of the soul. It is not this or that fragment of nature, which we have understood thoroughly that must lead us on. The whole enterprise of existence converges to spell out one unending wonder, one unbroken mystery. And man can draw close to the heart of that mystery, in those tense hours of love suffused with fear, when the creature responds to the Creator in the true acknowledgement of the privilege of his life.

In rejecting the hypothesis of scholasticism, Rabbi Judah restored religion to the common man's domain. In the Maimonidean conception, a sharp line was drawn between the few intellectually advanced members of the human race, and the great multitude of people. The snobbery of Greek thought was thus introduced into religion. Only those chosen few could attain the true ends of religion. For only the metaphysician, the man who had mastered the sciences, could rise to the love of God. The multitudes of humanity were doomed to live mediocre lives grasping only illusory goals. An impenetrable veil separated them from life's highest good—the realization of being at one with God. God's essence was eternal reason engaged in contemplating its own perfection, and only by the

FROM THE WORLD OF THE CABBALAH

way of reason could man draw close to Him. Rabbi Judah pushed this veil aside and summoned all men to draw close. They could enter through piety, through faith, through the doing of good deeds, through the study and practice of Torah, through the simple love and fear of their Maker.

Rabbi Judah was not unmindful of the peril to which the common man's piety was always exposed, its possible degradation into a habituated routine, into a formal exercise that was devoid of feeling. The degeneration of the study of Torah into a soulless play of the intellect, in which the sophistry of "pilpul" took the place of the sincere quest for truth, was the scandal of the age, and Rabbi Judah inveighed against it mercilessly. But all our spiritual endeavors may be corrupted by such distortions. Rabbi Judah pleaded for religious inwardness, and he sought to invest every religious act, in law or ritual, with profound significance. What was important, however, was the declaration of the common man's competence, the affirmation of a way that was open to all men by which they could draw close to their God.

Rabbi Judah's defense of the common man reckoned with the total human situation. It was not some abstraction from the larger context of life that was held up for commendation. Rabbi Judah was concerned not merely with man as a spirit, as a disembodied intelligence, but with man in the total aspects of his being. Thus Rabbi Judah rejected all morbidity about the material side of life, and he took his stand against the ascetics who identified the love of God with the need of rejecting the claims of a mundane existence. There is nothing in man that is inherently sinful. Man is a free agent, and he needs self-completion through a process of development. But whatever the Lord has put into his being, whether it is a drive for worldly goods or the hunger for sex-fulfillment, is intrinsically worthwhile. And his total life, above all when he has advanced on the path toward perfection, is eloquent testimony that whatever the Lord hath made is good.

This positive approach to man on the part of Rabbi Judah

included a recognition of his distinctive position in history. Rabbi Judah was impressed with the elements of universality, which all creatures have in common. But he discerned in all things elements of distinctiveness, of individuality, by which all creatures are differentiated from one another. In these he saw the special significance of their existence.

The differentiation of people into distinctive nations, which express themselves in distinctive cultures could not, therefore, be a casual appearance in history. It was part of the divine plan for the perfection of life. Thus he saw the unique facts of Jewish destiny, and the distinctive forms of Jewish culture as part of the divine plan. It was the fruit of God's initiative in history that had thus assigned to the Jewish people their specific vocation, to be the instrument for the dissemination of the principles of the Torah in the world, and help build unity in mankind by impregnating it with the awareness of the unity of God.

But here, too, Rabbi Judah was realistic. The Jews could not perform their vocation in a vacuum. The spirit must be carried by a physical base, and a community must be physically healthy if it is to cultivate spiritual values. It was for this reason that Rabbi Judah devoted so much attention to the physical problems of the Jewish group. It was necessary for the Jews to safeguard the elements that protect the group's capacity for survival in an alien environment, its distinctive diet, its distinctive group customs, its own language. Above all it must eventually attain its larger freedom, of being restored as a free nation, where, on its own distinctive territory, the true flowering of its genius might occur.

Rabbi Judah expressed himself in the idiom of his time. Many of his concepts are clearly Aristotelian. The influence of Aristotle on medieval culture was deep and far-reaching, and even those who rebelled against the basic elements of his thought, did not completely emancipate themselves from him. Thus Rabbi Judah's conception of time, his notion of a "natural place" which is distinctive to each organism, the assumed correspondence between cause and effect, the distinction between matter and form, the resolution of all substances to the four elements of fire, wind, water, earth, the four causes which precede each event in nature—all these derive ultimately from the teachings of Aristotle. That was a characteristic of the time, to criticize Aristotle and yet to continue, consciously or unconsciously, to employ the concepts which he had proclaimed in his doctrine.

Rabbi Judah derived his Aristotelian conceptions for the most part from Maimonides. He was a critic of many teachings of Maimonides, where he felt that they had yielded too much ground to the rationalists. But he acknowledged the authority of Maimonides not only in his expositions of Jewish law, but also in his philosophic works. Indeed, Rabbi Judah explained some of the concessions to rationalism on the part of Maimonides as an expedient of the time, made necessary in order to keep people from even greater yielding to Aristotelian ideas. Those concessions, Rabbi Judah felt, could not possibly represent the genuine position of Maimonides himself.

Many of Rabbi Judah's ideas are clearly neo-Platonic. His conception of "creation through privation," his doctrine of love as the underlying impulse which is at work throughout creation, his identification of the good as the vitalizing element which gives subsistence to all things, his conception of man as forging the world's unity by embodying within himself elements from the highest and lowest strata of existence, his conception of heaven and hell—all these reveal clearly the influence of neo-Platonism.

Whence did Rabbi Judah derive the influence of neo-Platonism? There had been a long tradition of neo-Platonism in Jewish thought. It was represented by Isaac Israeli, Ibn Gabirol, Bahya, Ibn Zaddik, Judah ha-Levi, Moses and Abraham Ibn Ezra, Nahmanides and Judah Abrabanel. The principal source of neo-Platonic ideas in Judaism was of course in the writings of the Cabbalah. In the early Middle Ages this trend was obscured by the towering genius of Maimonides, but now as the

FROM THE WORLD OF THE CABBALAH

Aristotelian influence receded, the neo-Platonists came into their own. Rabbi Judah was an adherent of the Cabbalah. He knew its major works, and he quoted them often.

Rabbi Judah was a forerunner of hasidism. The great masters of hasidic thought acknowledged him as one of the sources of their own inspiration. Thus Rabbi Simha Bunim hailed Rabbi Judah Loew as his teacher *par excellence,* whose writings had greatly enriched his own religious faith. He went on pilgrimages on Rabbi Loew's grave and even expressed the hope that he might be privileged to study under him in the spirit-world after death.[2]

Hasidism was a continuation of the Cabbalah, stripped only of some of its excesses in symbolism and transformed from a secret doctrine into a popular movement. The transformation of a new subtle theosophy into a mass movement was effected largely through the development within hasidism of the cult of the *Zaddik,* the holy master, about whom there organized a fellowship of disciples, and who served as an intermediary between the higher spiritual realms and the common people.

Rabbi Judah played an important role in this transformation. In his own idiom the ideas of the Cabbalah are presented with a minimum of that symbolic imagery in which the classic texts of the Cabbalah abound. These ideas, too, are developed toward a statement of faith and of discipline which can point the way of life for the common man in his spiritual dilemmas. For Rabbi Judah was not a writer for the chosen few. He stood in the midst of life and battled strenuously to give it direction and shape. Thus he helped prepare the way for the hasidic phase in Jewish mysticism.

Cultural movements seldom proceed in a straight line, to give immediate realization to the fullness of their promise. They often halt on the way or lose their course in some by-path, which proves unfruitful for future growth. Renaissance humanism, of which mysticism was a significant phase, took many diverse forms, but it moved toward one unfailing goal, which spelled the inauguration of the modern epoch in history.

FROM THE WORLD OF THE CABBALAH

The affirmation of individual experience as central in our quest for truth was at the core of its being. Its immediate achievement was the liberation of the individual from abstract universals and the focusing of interest on his own particular self. As it proceeded on its way, it brought with it all those elements which are the characteristic values of modern times, such as nationalism, democracy, a literature and art which is oriented to the individual man and his problems, and a system of education which is child-centered rather than text-centered. It brought with it also, as we have noted previously, the rise of modern science, for science too was born out of a concentration on particulars, rather than abstract universals. Its achievements in religion were no less striking. It inspired a shift of emphasis from the abstract problems of theology and metaphysics to man's need for faith with which to meet the crises of his own mundane life, a faith that would spell out its reality in the depths of his own inner experience.

Rabbi Judah represented the same movement in Judaism, though he naturally expressed it in his own idiom and applied it to the problems in his own milieu. He thus stands as a Jewish representative in the movement of transition from medieval to modern times.

PART I

THE WORLD OF THE CABBALAH

1 See Jacob B. Agus, "The Zohar", in *The Great Jewish Books,* New York, 1952, p. 197, and G. Scholem, *Major Trends in Jewish Mysticism,* Schocken, 1946, p. 157.
2 *Moreh Nebukim* III, 31.
3 *Moreh* I, 65; III, 32, 34.
4 *Major Trends in Jewish Mysticism,* pp. 213, 215.
5 *Zohar,* Idra Zuta, on Haazinu, p. 288a.
6 Mishnah, Hagigah 2:1.
7 Letter to Rabbi Solomon ben Abraham, in Jellinik's *Auswahl Kabbalistischer Mystik,* Leipzig, 1853, I pp. 13ff.
8 A brief survey of the literature of the Cabbalah appears in *Jewish Encyclopaedia* s. v. "Cabala", and in C. D. Ginsburg's *The Kabbalah,* Liverpool, 1865, pp. 65-123, 131-150. It is more elaborately treated in Gershon Scholem's *Major Trends in Jewish Mysticism.*
9 C. D. Ginsburg, *ibid.,* pp. 123-131, J. L. Blau, *The Christian Interpretation of the Cabala in the Renaissance,* New York, 1944.

PART II

A PORTRAIT OF THE MASTER

1 *D'rush l'Shabbat Teshubah,* ed. Warsaw, 1870. On the "nadler" calumny, see Isaac Rivkind, "Mishpete Kubyustusim", *Horeb,* Nisan 5695 II (1), pp. 60-66.
2 A descendant of Rabbi Judah, Meir Perles, wrote the first biography of his distinguished ancestor in 1718 under the title *Megillat Yuhasin* (Warsaw, 1864 and 1869). It is a brief chronicle of family traditions about Rabbi Judah's life and career. Another biography of Rabbi Judah was published in 1885 in Prague by Dr. Nathan Gruen under the title *Der Hohe Rabbi Loew.* There are also scattered shorter treatments of individual problems in the study of Rabbi Judah's life and work. A fresh examination of the scanty material we have about Rabbi Judah appears in the rather diffuse essay by A. Gottesdiener, "ha-Ari shebe-Hakme Prag", which was published in the Rabbi Kuk memorial volume (*Azkara,* Vol. III), in 1937.

[195]

FROM THE WORLD OF THE CABBALAH

[3] *Megillat Yuhasin*, ed. Warsaw, 1889, pp. 8, 17f. Dr. Gruen rejects the testimony of Perles and places the date of Rabbi Judah's birth after 1520. His grounds are circumstantial. Judah's elder brother, Hayim, was a pupil of the famous Polish scholar, Rabbi Shakhna. Moses Iserles was then his fellow-student. Since Iserles was born in 1520, we must assume that Hayim was born approximately at the same time. Judah, who was Hayim's younger brother, must therefore have been born after 1520. But clearly Hayim and Iserles need not have been of the same age, and there is no reason to invalidate the testimony of Perles. See Gruen, *ibid*, pp. 6-7, and A. Gottesdiener, *ibid*, pp. 267-268. According to Perles, Judah was "the first to rebel against pilpul".

[4] Among the Cabbalistic works cited by Rabbi Judah are the *Sefer Yezirah*, *Maareket ha-Elohut* (Mantua 1558), *Abodat ha-Kodesh* by Meir ibn Gabbai (1531), the *Sefer ha-Bahir*, and of course the *Zohar*. See *Beer ha-Golah*, pp. 17, 28, 83, 86, 88, 137; *Nezah Yisrael*, ch. 34; *Tiferet Yisrael*, ch. 65; *Geburot her-Shem*, ch. 68; *Derek ha-Hayim*, Warsaw 1876, pp. 11a, 39b, 50b, 82a-83b, 88b, 89a-90b, 98a; *Netibot Olam*, Torah 9, 14, Abodah 12, 16, Teshubah 8; *Hidushe Gur Arye* on Shabbat 10b, 31b. Cf. Gottesdiener, *ibid*., pp. 270, 290-307.

[5] According to Perles (*ibid*., p. 18) Judah was sent by his future father-in-law to study under Rabbi Solomon Luria, but a reversal in circumstances put an end to these plans.

[6] Mishnah Abot 5:21 prescribes the age for marriage as eighteen, but in practice it was usually earlier.

[7] *Megillat Yuhasin*, p. 24.

[8] Ernest Cassirer, "Some Remarks on the Question of the Originality of the Renaissance", *Journal of the History of Ideas*, IV, pp. 54-55; J. H. Randall, *The Making of the Modern Mind*, Cambridge, 1926, pp. 111-248; H. O. Taylor, *Thought and Expression in the Sixteenth Century* (2 volumes); John Calvin, *Institutes*, Book I, ch. VII.

[9] See Frank Rosenthal, "The Rise of Christian Hebraism in the 16th Century", *Historia Judaica*, VII 2 (Oct. 1945), pp. 167-191; Erwin J. Rosenthal, "Sebastian Muenster's Knowledge and Use of Jewish Exegesis", in *Essays Presented to J. H. Hertz* (London, 1942), pp. 351-369, and S. Stein, "Phillipus Ferdinandus Polonus", *ibid*., pp. 397-412; *Takanot Medinot Mehrin* (Hebrew), edited by I. Heilprin, Jerusalem, 1952, pp. 57-59; Preserved Smith, *Erasmus*, New York, 1923, p. 48; Previte Orton, *Cambridge Medieval History*, Vol. III, p. 805.

[10] Rabbi Judah ben Bezalel, *D'rush al ha-Torah*, Warsaw, 1836, p. 25a; Gottesdiener, *ibid*., pp. 256-265; Gutmann Klemperer, "The Rabbis of Prague", in *Historia Judaica*, XIII (1950), pp. 33-66; Bruno Blau, "Nationality among Czechoslovak Jewry", *ibid*., X 2, 1948, p. 148; Paul Nettl, *The Story of Dance Music*, New York, 1947, pp. 41f; Tobias Jakobovitz, "Die Juedische Zunfte in Prag," in *Gesellschaft fuer Geschichte der Juden in der Czechoslov. Republik*,

VIII, pp. 57-131; S. Dubnow, *History of the Jews in Russia and Poland*, Philadelphia, 1918, Vol. I, pp. 1-121. E. M. Wiebur, in *A History of Unitarianism*, pp. 238ff, surmises that Catherine had indeed been a convert to Judaism. L. D. Barnett, in "Two Documents of the Inquisition", *Jewish Quarterly Review*, N. S. XV (1924-5) pp. 214f, tells of a Friar Diogo da Asumsao who was burned in 1603 for rejecting Catholicism in favor of Judaism. C. Roth, in "Aboab's Proselytization of Marranos", *ibid.*, XXIII 2 (1932), pp. 121-163, tells of a French nobleman who embraced Judaism in 1575. Cf. also Roland H. Bainton, "Sebastian Castello and the Toleration Controversy of the Sixteenth Century", in *Persecution and Liberty*, pp. 183-203.

[11] Charles Singer, "Historical Relations of Religion and Science," in *Science, Religion and Reality*, edited by Joseph Needham, New York, 1928, pp. 87-131; B. Suller, "Ein Maimonides-Streit in sechzehnten Jahrhundert," *Jahrbuch der Gesellschaft fuer Geschichte der Juden in der Czechoslov. Republik*, VIII, pp. 412ff.

[12] Bruno Blau, *ibid.*, Guido Kisch, "Linguistic Conditions among Czechoslovak Jewry," *ibid.*, VIII (1946), pp. 19-32; S. Baron. *The Jewish Community*, Philadelphia, 1942, II, pp. 20f; Rabbi Judah Loew ben Bezalel, *D'rush al ha-Torah*, Warsaw, 1836, p. 25a; Gottesdiener, *ibid.*, pp. 258f. Cf. Gabriel Compayre, *Abelard*, New York, 1893, p. 189.

[13] See Gottesdiener, *ibid.*, pp. 273-290, 304-345; David Ganz, s. v. Rabbi Liva, Mordecai Jaffee; *Takanot Medinat Mehrin*, pp. 59, 60, note 1; Haim-Yair Bachrach in *Havath Yair*, No. 123; Rabbi Judah ben Bezalel, *D'rush al ha-Mizvot*, Warsaw, 1836, pp. 27a-32a; *D'rush l'Shabbat 'ha-Gadol*, p. 38a; *D'rush l'Shabbat Teshubah*, p. 5a, 9a; *Nezah Yisrael*, ch. 25; *Gur Arye*, Mishpatim; *Netibot*, Abodah 12, ha-Din 1, 2, Anavah, 5, 6, 7; *Derek ha-Hayim*, pp. 15a-17a, 66b-67a, 90b. The division among scholars into hostile camps on the question of "pilpul" is alluded to by David Ganz, *ibid.*, s. v. Rabbi Jacob Pollack.

Part III

HUMAN DESTINY

[1] Y. Rosenberg, *Niflaot ha-Maharal*, Warsaw, 1909; Chaim Bloch, *The Golem*, Vienna, 1923; Gottesdiener, *ibid.*, pp. 348-353.

[2] Sanhedrin 65b; Joshua Trachtenberg, *Jewish Magic and Superstition*, New York 1939, pp. 84ff; Sh. M. Chones, *Toldot ha-Poskim*, Warsaw, 1922, p. 67, *Jewish Encyclopaedia*, s. v. Golem; Pachter, *Paracelsus*, New York, 1951, pp. 14f; *Cyclopaedia of Biblical, Theological and Ecclesiastical Literature*, New York, 1878, s. v. Albertus Magnus.

[3] *Beer ha-Golah*, pp. 21-24. Cf. also *Gur Arye* on *Ki Thiso*, pp. 368-369 where Rabbi Judah holds that the golden calf had been animated by magic.

FROM THE WORLD OF THE CABBALAH

4 G. Scholem, *Major Trends in Jewish Mysticism*, p. 99 and his article "golem" in *Encyclopaedia Judaica; Shomer Emunim*, Berlin, 1927, p. 4b.

5 Lincoln Barnett, *The Universe and Dr. Einstein*, New York, 1948, p. 108.

6 Rabbi Judah assumes throughout his writings this principle of correspondence that must necessarily prevail between cause and effect. It is ultimately an Aristotelian doctrine, and it is discussed by Maimonides, but he had suggested that this principle holds only where the cause produces the effect by natural necessity, rather than by a free act of will. See B. Bokser, *The Legacy of Maimonides*, New York, 1950, pp. 33f.

7 See I. Husik, *A History of Jewish Philosophy*, New York, 1930, pp. 178, 233, 403 and G. Scholem, *Major Trends in Jewish Mysticism*, pp. 38f.

8 *Derek ha-Hayim*, pp. 8b-11b, 34a, 46a-46b, 48a, 49b-50b, 51a-56b, 58a-60a, 63b, 82a-83b, 84b-85a (ch. 5), 88a, 90a, 97b-98b, 119b-121a, 124a; *Netibot Olam*, Torah 1, 2, Gemilut Hasadim 5, Lezanut 1, ha-Lashon 1, 2, ha-Perishut 1, Bitahon, Ayin Tob, Temimut 1; *Ner Mizvah*, pp. 80a-81a, 84b, 85b; *Geburot ha-Shem*, ch. 4, 5, 8, 9, 23, 40, 41, 44, 46, 54, 55, 60, 65, 67, 69, 70, 71; *Tiferet Yisrael*, Introduction, ch. 1, 2, 7, 11, 12, 16, 17, 24, 25, 33, 37, 50, 55, 69, 70; *Nezah Yisrael*, ch. 1, 3, 4, 5, 21, 22; *Or Hadash* (Warsaw, 1872), p. 5; *Beer ha-Golah*, pp. 35, 53, 83-88, 102, 119; *D'rush l'Shabbat ha-Gadol*, pp. 19b-20a; *D'rush l'Shabbat Teshubah*, pp. 5a, 7b; *Hidushe Gur Arye* on Shabbat 31a, 31b; *Gur Arye* on Toldot p. 117, Haye Sarah pp. 111f, Shemot p. 225, Vaero p. 225, Bo pp. 250, 259, Jethro p. 300, Vayikra p. 16, Kedoshim p. 39, Shelah p. 189, Hukat pp. 215f, Balak p. 222.

The concept of the universe as an integrated unity is familiar in Jewish thought, Cf. Maimonides, *Moreh*, I 72. The metaphor comparing existence to a tree appears often in the Cabbalah, as indicated by G. Scholem, in *Major Trends in Jewish Mysticism*, p. 23. Rabbi Judah's estimate of man follows the general concepts taught in the various writings of the Cabbalah. For the estimate of man, cf. also Calvin, *ibid.*, ch. V 3. Marsilio Ficino assigns to the soul the significance which Rabbi Judah ascribes to man as a whole, but, like Rabbi Judah, extols man as a kind of God in relation to the order of life below him. Rabbi Judah's estimate of man is paralleled in the writings of Pico della Mirandola. See Ficino's *Platonic Theology*, III 2; XIII, 2; XIV, 3, translated by J. L. Burroughs and published in *Journal of History of Ideas*, V 2 (April, 1944), pp. 223-238 and Paul Oskar Kristeller, *The Philosophy of Marsilio Ficino*, New York, 1943, pp. 407-410. It is also paralleled in the writings of Paracelsus. See his *Selected Writings*, New York, 1951, pp. 112, 117, 119, 169, 273. Cf. G. Scholem, *Major Trends in Jewish Mysticism*, pp. 67-70, 140. The denial of original sin, as the hereditary effect of Adam's fall appears also in Hasdai Crescas. See his "Bitul ikre dat ha-Nozrim" in J. Eisenstein's *Ozar Vikuhim*, p. 298.

FROM THE WORLD OF THE CABBALAH

9 *Netibot Olam,* Torah, ch. 15, Lezanut, ch. 1; *Derek Ha-Hayim* 32a-33a; *Tiferet Yisrael,* ch. 2, 3; *Gur Arye* on Vayeze; *D'rush al ha-Torah,* ed. Warsaw, 1836, pp. 5b-6b; *D'rush l'Shabbat ha-Gadol,* p. 37b; *Or Hadash,* Introduction. Cf. the interpretation of Gen. 8:21 as "For the nature of man is evil because of his youth" rather than "*from* his youth" in *Akedat Yishak* by Isaac Arama, Noah, 13, and see also Maimonides, *Moreh* III 22.

10 *Derek ha-Hayim,* 41b-43a, 56b-57a; *D'rush l'Shabbat ha-Gadol,* pp. 18b-19a, 33a-33b; *Netibot,* Koah ha-Yezer, ch. 4.

11 *Netibot,* Torah, 2, 4, 10, Abodah 16, Koah ha-Yezer 3, Osher 2, Shalom 3, Anavah 6; *Geburot ha-Shem,* ch. 43, 51; *Derek ha-Hayim* 13a, 13b, 26a-28a, 38b-40b, 47a, 48a-49a, 58b-60a, 100b. *Tiferet Yisrael,* ch. 24, 25; *Or Hadash* 5b; *Beer ha-Golah* Introduction 2, pp. 29-32, 65, 67, 92, 106. Cf. Kristeller, *ibid.,* ch. 14 for the views of Ficino, who expounded a doctrine of asceticism. Rabbi Judah's high esteem for man is in Ficino limited to the soul. Rabbi Judah's rejection of asceticism and his appreciation of marriage follows the formulation in the Cabbalah, and here Jewish mysticism differs from its Christian counterpart. See G. Scholem, *ibid.,* p. 235.

12 *Netibot,* Yirat ha-Shem, Ahabat ha-Shem; *Nezah Yisrael,* ch. 29; *Derek ha-Hayim,* pp. 11b-12a; *Gur Arye,* on Shabbat 31a.

13 *Netibot,* Torah, 3, 14, Ahabat Rea, 1, 2, Zedakah, 5, Anavah, 3, 7, Shalom, 1, 2, 3; *Derek ha-Hayim,* pp. 14a-15a, 21a-23b, 37a-38b, 63b; *D'rush l'Shabbat Teshubah,* p. 56; *D'rush l'Shabbat ha-Gadol,* pp. 24b-25a; *Or Hadash,* p. 8a.

14 *D'rush al Torah,* pp. 21ff; *Netibot,* Emet, Ahabat Rea 3, Shalom 3; *Beer ha-Golah,* pp. 13, 150-152; *Derek ha-Hayim,* 17b-19a, 38b-40a, 97b-100b; *Geburot ha-Shem,* ch. 19. On the attitude toward idolatry, cf. also John Calvin, *Institutes,* Book I, ch. III 1. Pico della Mirandola taught similarly that all philosophies share a common universal truth. See Paul Oskar Kristeller, "The Philosophy of Man in the Italian Renaissance", in *Italia,* XXIV 2 (June 1947), p. 103.

15 *D'rush l'Shabbat ha-Gadol,* pp. 13b, 17b, 38a; *D'rush l'Shabbat Teshubah,* p. 5a; *Netibot,* Anavah, 5, 6, 7, Kaas, 2, Zeniut 3, Gemilut Hasadim, 1, 5, Zedakah, 4, *Gur Arye* Bereshit; *Beer ha-Golah,* pp. 8, 24f, 147f; *Nezah Yisrael,* ch. 1, 39; *Geburot ha-Shem,* ch. 8, 35, 36, 42, 45, 46; *Or Hadash,* pp. 8b, 9a, 44b, 45b, 48a; *Derek ha-Hayim,* 21a-23b, 31a-32a, 47a. The strictures against the state and especially his conception of government are of great interest. Abravanel disliked the political order as an "artificial" infringement of human life, and he denounced absolutist government, especially an absolute king. He interpreted Deut. XVII, 14f as optional, unlike most Jewish commentators who took those verses as a command to establish a monarchy. Nevertheless, he assigned a much more exalted position to the king than did Rabbi Judah. In forbidding rebellion against a king, even when he rules unjustly, Abravanel regards the king as representing God, as the image of God. The

FROM THE WORLD OF THE CABBALAH

king parallels God's absolute power and unity, his extra-legal actions corresponding to God's miracles, and his unique position in the universe. See his commentary on Deut. 17, 16-20, I Kings 2:37-12:2, and cf. L. Strauss, "On Abravanel's Philosophical Tendency and Political Teaching" in *Isaac Abravanel*, Cambridge, 1937. Cf. also Ibn Vergase's *Shebet Yehudah*, ed. Wiener, p. 21, where the statement occurs: "In essence the nation is the king; the king is sovereign in name." Cf. H.M. Pachter, *Paracelsus* (New York, 1951), pp. 201f, who notes in Paracelsus a somewhat similar conception of the uniqueness of individuals and of national communities. The conception of evil as the disharmony created because something which is good in its rightful place has violated some balance and encroached upon a domain which is not its own, is taught by Joseph Gikatila and some other Cabbalists, but it is differently treated in the *Zohar*. See G. Scholem, *ibid.*, p. 225.

[16] *Beer ha-Golah*, pp. 146-150; *Gur Arye*, Beshalah; *Netibot*, Ahabat Rea 1, 2; ha-Lashon, Abodah 14, 1-11, ha-Shetikah, 1, Koah ha-Yezer, 1, Zedakah, 4, 5; *Derek ha-Hayim*, pp. 14a-15a, 21a-23b, 31a-32a, 41b-43a, 48a-49a, 63a-63b, 68a, 74b-75a, 77a-77b, 96b-97a; *Nezah Yisrael*, ch. 7.

[17] *Beer ha-Golah*, pp. 55-8, 79-81, 102; *Netibot*, Torah 1, Koah ha-Yezer 3; *D'rush l'Shabbat Teshubah*, pp. 6a, 6b; *D'rush l'Shabbat ha-Gadol*, pp. 12b ff, 17a, 17b; *Derek ha Hayim*, 24a-26a, 57b-60a, 63a-63b, 82a, 83b, 105b-107a; 124b; *Geburot ha-Shem*, ch. 64.

PART IV

REASON AND FAITH

[1] The principal critic of Aristotle in Jewish thought who also influenced the trend away from Aristotle in general culture, was Hasdai Crescas. See H. A. Wolfson, *Cresca's Critique of Aristotle*, Cambridge, 1929. For a discussion of the major representatives of the Aristotelian tradition in Jewish thought, see Isaac Husik, *A History of Jewish Philosophy*, New York, 1930. On Azariah dei Rossi, see I. Zinberg, *Geschichte der Literatur bei Yidn* (Yiddish), Vilna, 1933, vol. IV, pp. 143-153, 473, 474. The accusation that rationalists have proven disloyal to the Jewish people and an easy prey to Christian propaganda is made by Shem Tob ben Shem Tob in his *Sefer Emunot*, p. 4a and also by Joseph ben Hayim Javitz, in his *Orah Hayim*, 5, p. 12. The complaint that rationalists are indifferent to Jewish piety is voiced with much feeling by Menahem ben Abraham ben Zerah in the introduction to his *Zedah la-Derek*. Cf. also Elijah del Medigo, *Behinat ha-Dat*, 72. Rabbi Judah's reaction to the *Meor Enayim* are given in *Beer ha-Golah*, section 6, end.

[2] *Beer ha-Golah*, pp. 47ff, 59-62, 65, 79-81, 103; *Geburot ha-Shem*, Introduction, ch. 46, 52; *Tiferet Yisrael*, ch. 6, 65; *Netibot*, Torah, 14, Ahabat Rea, 2, Gemilut Hasadim, 4; *Nezah Yisrael*, ch. 6; *D'rush l'Shabbat ha-Gadol*, p. 33b; *Derek ha-Hayim*, Introduction, pp. 43b-44a, 82a-83b.

3 *Tiferet Yisrael*, ch. 4, 6, 9, 10, 11, 12; *Derek ha-Hayim*, p. 21b; *Geburot ha-Shem*, Introduction, ch. 34. Not all "philosophers" ignored morality. Maimonides, for instance, made the moral life a prerequisite for intellectual perfection, but Maimonides had clearly underestimated the moral life in comparison with the intellectual. Morality was important only in so far as it affected a person's intellectual powers. By itself, it could not bring a man close to God. In some of the disciples of Maimonides the eclipse of morality by reason was even more complete. See B. Z. Bokser, *The Legacy of Maimonides*, New York, 1950, pp. 20ff, 44. The view that the celestial bodies are living beings, possessed of souls, is challenged also by Saadia, Judah ha-Levi, Crescas, and Isaac Arama. See H. A. Wolfson, *Philo*, I, p. 418. Cf. Joseph ben David Yahia who in his *Torah Or* (Bologna, 1538), criticizes Maimonides for limiting immortality to the intellectually developed on the ground that most people would thus be excluded from life's highest good.

4 *Netibot*, Kaas, 1; *Geburot ha-Shem*, Introduction, ch. 25, 55; *Beer ha-Golah*, pp. 22f, 75; *Derek ha-Hayim*, pp. 33b, 51a-56b, 63b (ch. 4), 73a, 89a-92a, 121a. Rabbi Judah is explicit in his criticism of Gersonides with whose views on miracles he deals at length. He attacked him especially for reading his radical ideas into the Bible: "He devised interpretations devoid of any sense and meaning. Only the merit of the prophets was of help in that his interpretation sounds so far-fetched that whoever sees or hears it rejects it." (*Geburot ha-Shem*, Introduction). Rabbi Judah ascribed to Maimonides the theory that specific miracles were provided for in the original act of creation. He probably based this on his Mishnah commentary, Eight Chapters, ch. 8, but in *Moreh* II 29 the final view of Maimonides is that God acts with complete freedom of initiative, which makes possible temporary modifications in natural law. According to Judah ben Isaac Abrabanel the identification of God with reason is Aristotelian, while the view that reason is only one of God's creations is Platonic. See Zinberg, *ibid.*, IV, p. 27. Crescas als fought the intellectualization of Judaism maintaining that man can rise to the love of God, to the benefits of divine providence as well as to immortality though the performance of the commandments in the Torah, without intellectual perfection. The need for the physical performance of the commandments derives from the physical dimension of man's existence. See Emanuel Joel, *Torat ha-Filosofia ha-Datit shel Rabi don Hasdai Crescas*, Tel Aviv, 1928, pp. 80-86. This was substantially the view of Rabbi Judah ha-Levi. See I. Epstein, "Judah ha-Levi as a Philosopher", *Jewish Quarterly Review*, N. S. XXV 3, pp. 223f.

5 *Geburot ha-Shem*, ch. 7, 8, 9, 45, 46; *Tiferet Yisrael*, Introduction, ch. 1, 3-9, 16, 18, 26, 32, 35, 50, 61; 62, *Netibot*, Torah, 1, 2, 15, Abodah, 1, 2 Zeniut; *Beer ha-Golah*, pp. 28, 29, 118, 119, 120, 133; *Gur Arye* on Jethro; *D'rush l'Shabbat Teshubah*, pp. 2b, 8b; *Derek ha-Hayim*, Introduction 8b, 9a; Rabbi Judah follows closely on Joseph Albo's formulation of three principles fundamental to all religion as well as in his distinction between a natural,

FROM THE WORLD OF THE CABBALAH

conventional, and divine law. Cf. *Ikkarim,* I ch. 7-11. It is interesting that while Luther's disparagement of the body led him to disparage the tools by which the body fulfills its destiny, he saw a value in works to honor God, to correspond to man's bodily nature. See Taylor, *Thought and Expression in the Sixteenth Century,* Vol. 1, pp. 225-228. Sebastian Castello also taught that the fundamental elements of ethics inhere in human nature. See "Sebastian Castello and the Toleration Controversy of the Sixteenth Century," by R. H. Bainton in *Persecution and Liberty,* pp. 191-5. Cf. John Calvin, *Institutes,* Book I, ch. III 2, 3, VIII, who inveighs similarly against the notion that the Bible is a human work, and that religion was "devised by the cunning and craft of a few individuals, as a means of keeping the body of the people in due subjection." It is interesting that even Pomponazzi, who is normally regarded as an Aristotelian, likewise rejected speculative reason as the distinctive essence of man, and he regarded moral virtue rather than contemplation as the way of man's highest end. See Paul Oskar Kristeller, "The Philosophy of Man in the Italian Renaissance", in *Italia,* XXIV 2 (June 1947), pp. 106-109.

6 *Tiferet Yisrael,* ch. 33, 63, 64, 65, 66, 68; *Beer ha-Golah,* pp. 9, 60, 62, 63; *Gur Arye* on Gen. 6:6 and on Jethro; *Nezah Yisrael,* ch. 9; *Geburot ha-Shem,* ch. 23, 25, 29. Rabbi Judah's interpretation of Biblical anthropomorphisms appears in other Cabbalistic works. Cf. G. Scholem, *Major Trends in Jewish Mysticism,* pp. 224, 402, n. 66.

7 *Tiferet Yisrael,* Introduction, ch. 6, 7, 13, ch. 24, 25, 33, 40, 50, 51, 55, 70; *Geburot ha-Shem,* Introduction (2), ch. 9, 13, 23, 26, 46, 54, 58, 60, 69, 70, 71; *Nezah Yisrael,* ch. 1, 21, 22; *Gur Arye* on Bereshit, p. 25, Shemot p. 220, Noah p. 58, Shelah p. 189, Hukat p. 215f, Balak p. 222, Vaethanan p. 277; *D'rush al ha-Torah,* pp. 9a, 14a; *Beer ha-Golah,* pp. 21, 22, 141-143; *Derek ha-Hayim,* pp. 39b, 88b, 98a; *Hidushe Gur Arye* on Shabbat 35b. See *Sefer Yizerah,* 112 and cf. J. Abelson, *Jewish Mysticism,* London, 1913, ch. 5. Cf. C. D. Ginsburg, *The Kabbalah,* London, 1865, p. 65-78 and J. Tishbe, *Mishnat ha-Zohar,* Jerusalem, 1949, pp. 144-148. For the same approach to Biblical exegesis in the writings of Reuchlin see Ginsburg, *ibid.,* pp. 126-131. On the significance of the middle element in the series, cf. Paul Oskar Kristeller, *The Philosophy of Marsilio Ficino,* New York, 1943, pp. 92-120.

8 W. Monroe, *Comenius and the Beginning of Educational Reform,* Scribner's, 1900; Taylor, *Thought and Expression in the Sixteenth Century,* Vol. I, pp. 161ff, 211, 377-381, 387-388. Cf. Joseph Irgas, *Shomer Emunim,* Berlin, 1927, p. 15b.

9 *Derek ha-Hayim,* ed. Warsaw, 1876, pp. 116b-117b; *Netibot,* Torah 5, 10; Zerizut, 1; *D'rush al-ha-Mitzvot; Gur Arye,* Vaethanan; *D'rush al ha-Torah,* Warsaw, 1836, Introduction, pp. 20a-end.

10 *Netibot,* Tokakah, 3; *D'rush al ha-Torah, ibid.*

11 *Gur Arye,* Vaethanan; *D'rush al ha-Torah, ibid.*

FROM THE WORLD OF THE CABBALAH

12 *Tiferet Yisrael*, ch. 56; *Gur Arye, ibid*.
13 *Derek ha-Hayim, ibid*.; *D'rush al ha-Torah, ibid*.
14 Cited by S. Asaf, *Mekorot l'Toldot ha-Hinuk b'Yisrael*, Tel-Aviv, 1925, I pp. 43, 53.
15 *Netibot*, Torah 10, 15, Zerizut, 1; *D'rush al ha-Torah, ibid*.; *Gur Arye, ibid*.; *Tiferet Yisrael, ibid*.; Yom Tob Lippman Heller, *Tosefot Yom Tob*, Introduction.
16 *D'rush al ha-Torah, ibid*.; *Netibot*, Torah, 10.

PART V
JUDAISM AND CHRISTIANITY

1 See above, pp. 25f and see Ch. Bloch, *The Golem*, pp. 53-63; *Hokmat Maharal*, Pieterkov, 1911, pp. 4-58; Zinberg, *Die Geschichte fin der Literatur*, Vol. IV, pp. 470f.
2 *D'rush al ha-Torah*, pp. 24a-25b; *Gur Arye, Vayehi* (p. 202), Shoftim (p. 316).
3 *Tiferet Yisrael*, ch. 18, 57, 58, 59; *Nezah Yisrael*, ch. 30; *Netibot*, Torah 15, Abodah 9, Anavah 3, Ahabat Rea 1, Zeniut 4, Tokakah 1, Lezanut 2, Kaas 2; *Derek ha-Hayim*, pp. 12b-14a, 75a-75b, 103a-104a; *Geburot ha-Shem*, Introduction, ch. 34, 46, 47. Cf. Albo, *Ikkarim* III ch. 25.
4 *Tiferet Yisrael*, ch. 46, 49, 50, 51, 52, 53, 64. Cf. Albo, *ibid*.
5 *Tiferet Yisrael*, ch. 51; *Nezah Yisrael*, ch. 11; *Geburot ha-Shem*, ch. 24, 67, 72.
6 *Nezah Yisrael*, ch. 2, 3, 10, 14, 15, 18, 19, 22, 32, 56; *Geburot ha-Shem*, ch. 8, 9, 39, 60; *D'rush l'Shabbat Teshubah*, pp. 11b, 12a.
7 *Nezah Yisrael*, ch. 1, 6, 10, 24, 25; *Ner Mitzvah*, p. 85b; *D'rush al ha-Mitzvot*, pp. 27b-88b; *Geburot ha-Shem*, ch. 24, 66, 70; G. A. Kayre, "Galileo and Plato", *Journal of the History of Ideas*, Oct. 1943, pp. 408-411 and Edgar Zilsel, "Copernicus and Mechanics", *ibid*., Jan. 1940, pp. 115f; *Beer ha-Golah*, p. 148.
8 *Or Hadash*, p. 8a, 15a; *Ner Mizvah*, 80-80b, 84, 84b; *Nezah Yisrael*, ch. 26, 27, 29, 35, 36, 42; *Gur Arye* on Bo (p. 262); *Geburot ha-Shem*, ch. 18, 34, 46, 52; Ibn Gabirol, *Mekor Hayim*, 5:31, and cf. Plato's *Phaedo*; Paracelsus, *Selected Works*, pp. 217f.
9 *Beer ha-Golah*, Introduction.
10 *Ibid*., ch. 1; *Gur Arye*, on Jethro.
11 *Beer ha-Golah*, ch 2, 3, 4, 5.
12 *Ibid*., ch. 6. Cf. *Nezah Yisrael*, ch. 5.
13 *Beer ha-Golah*, ch. 7.

PART VI
THE LEGACY OF RABBI JUDAH

1 A. N. Whitehead, *Science and the Modern World*, New York, 1926, p. 12.
2 *Simhat Yisrael*, Pieterkov, 1902, p. 30 sec. 68, p. 131, sec. 335.

INDEX

Abigdor—36, 37
Abrabanel, Judah—192
Abraham—131
Abraham ibn Ezra—19, 192
Abulafia, Abrahan ben Samuel—8, 9, 10
academies—138, 139
Acquinas, Thomas—57
Active Intellect—109, 110, 117
Adam—63
Agadah—98, 101, 181
Albalag—100
Albo, Joseph—19, 158
alchemists—56
Aleman, Johanan—11
allegory—118
alphabet, Hebrew—7
Altneuschul—38, 47
am ha-aretz—182
angels—64, 67
anthropomorphism—121, 123
anti-semitism—151, 153
Apocrypha—97
Aristotle—2, 3, 31, 75, 100-102, 109, 113, 130, 134, 172, 187, 188
Aristotelian—110, 174, 191
asceticism—60, 73, 74
Ashkenazi, Eliezer, Rabbi—42
asmakhta—179
assimilation—32
astronomy—20, 98, 104
Atonement, Day of—164
Austria—28
Azariah—98
Azariel—7

Baal Shem Tob, Israel, Rabbi—57
Bachrach, Samuel, Rabbi—45
Bacon—31
Bahir—10
Bahya—192

Basel—154
Bavaria—28
Beer ha-Golah—48, 149, 156, 178
Birkat ha-Minim—183
Bergson, Henri—12
Bezalel—18, 20, 49
Bible—31, 56, 69, 101, 139, 143, 157, 161, 165, 179
Biblical law—165, 179, 180
Biblical narratives—2, 3
Biblical prophecies—157
Bloch, Chaim—58
Bohemia—28, 30, 33
Bohemian Jews—28, 32
Brahe—31
Bruno—31
Bunim, Simha, Rabbi—193

Cabbalah—1, 2, 4, 6, 7, 8, 10, 11, 13, 25, 26, 37, 42, 43, 47, 56, 57, 58, 64, 68, 98, 111, 120, 129, 135, 153, 187, 193
Cabbalah, Christian—11, 12
Cabbalism—128
Cabbalists—4-6, 11, 57, 60, 76, 127, 128, 131, 171
Calvin, John—158
Cardobero, Moses—11
Caro, Joseph—99, 143
casuistry—135, 141
Catalonia—8
Catholicism—28
causality—113, 182
censorship—153
character—71, 72
charity—87, 88
chess—137
Chmielnicki—12
Christian—8, 32, 74, 129, 131, 142, 151, 152, 157, 158, 162
Christiani, Pablo—8

[205]

Christianity—37, 152, 153, 155, 156, 158, 161, 163, 165, 182
Church, Catholic—23
circumcision—95
cities—91
code, moral—116, 117
codes—143
collective reason—117
Cologne—20, 49
Comenius—135
commandments — 106, 118-120, 126, 164
Commentary on the Ten Sefirot—7
contentiousness—82
controversy—83
Copernicus—20, 22, 31, 104, 172
Cracow—30, 46
creation—116, 176
creation through opposites—175
Creator—66, 177
creatures—89-91
Crescas, Hasdai—20, 158

Daud, Ibn—100
De Arte Cabalistica—11
De Meschia Disputatio—154
De Verbo Mirifico—11
deficiency—145
democracy—194
Derek ha-Hayim—47, 53, 95
destiny, Jewish—191
determinism—113
diaspora—167
dictators—183
dignity, human—87, 88, 89, 159
discussion—142
dispersion—172, 173
disputation—8
dissent—83
divine image—68
divorce—75

earth—109
education—34, 44, 45, 135, 137, 140, 141, 142, 194
education, abuses in—34, 137
Elazar—95
Eliezer, of Worms—11
Elijah, of Chelm—57
Empire, Holy Roman—23, 29
En Sof—4
Erasmus—26
Eretz Yisrael—172
ethics—120
Etz Hayim—10
evil—62, 63, 70, 74
evil impulse—70, 71, 72
excommunication—18, 41, 99
existence, unity of—60, 61, 62, 64, 66, 92
exile—172, 173, 174, 176
Ezekiel—6
Ezra—7

faith—190
Falaquera, Shem Tob—11
Faust—57
female—75
Ferrara—97
feudalism—22
Fons Vitae—175
Forster, Johannes—25
France—33
Frederick, III—11
free will—70
freedom—67, 85, 86, 149, 173, 174

Gabirol, Solomon ibn—57, 175, 192
Galileo—31
Ganz, David—36, 153
Geburot ha-Shem—46
Germany—33
Gerona—8
Gersonides—19, 100
Ginzberg, Akiba—48
God—1, 3-5, 7, 9, 12, 23, 42, 44, 55, 56, 59, 64, 65, 67, 68, 70, 71, 74,

77, 78, 85, 90, 91, 100, 105-107, 110-113, 115, 116, 121, 122, 124, 129, 152, 165, 175, 181, 183, 187-189
God, fear of—77, 78
God, glorification of—91
God, love of—77, 78
Goethe—57
golem—55, 58, 128
good—192
good deeds—190
grammar—142
Greek philosophers—20
Greek thought—3, 189
Greeks—2
Guide to the Perplexed—37, 75
Gur Arye—46

Haman—87
Hanukkah—124, 180
harmony—84
Hasidism—1, 11-13, 57, 135, 193
heaven and hell—160
hebra mishnayot—143
Hebraists, Christian—25, 154
Hebrew—34, 127, 128, 142, 153
hell—159, 160
Heller, Yom Tob Lippman—38, 143
hereafter—159, 160, 162
Hayim ben Bezalel—19, 142
Hayot, Isaac, Rabbi—18, 38, 45, 46
heresy, "Judaizing"—26
Hidushe Gur Arye—49
Hokmat ha-Nefesh—11
Holy Aged—5, 6
Holy Land—9
humanism—22, 193
humanists—26, 134, 153
Huss, John—28

idolators—183
idolatry—81, 105
Igeret ha-Kodesh—75

immortality—108
individual—83
inwardness—190
Institutes—158
Intelligences—100, 108, 109, 111
Intellect—109, 113
Irgas, Joseph—57
Isaac the Blind—7
Isaiah—6, 122
Israel—10, 165, 166, 167, 169
Israeli, Isaac—192
Italy—33

Jaffe, Mordecai, Rabbi—48
Jerusalem—98, 163
Jesus—151, 154-157, 162, 163, 165
Jesuits—153
Jewish unity—174
Jews—8, 24, 26, 29, 163, 167, 168, 169, 174
Jews—calumny against—151
Jews, expulsion of—27, 29
Jews, hostility toward—25
Jews, in Persia—86
Jews, persecutions of—18
Jews, sufferings of—10, 163, 167, 169
Josippon—20
Judah ha-Levi—192
Judah Loew ben Bezalel—13, 17-49
Judaism—1, 28, 152, 153, 183
Judaism, attacks against—152
judges—91
justice—84, 87

Karo, Menahem—36
Kimhi—19
king—84, 85, 91
Klaus synagog—38, 56
knowledge—112

law—42, 158, 162, 164, 180
law, abrogation of—42, 162
law, natural—118

legends—101
Lemberg—49
Leon, Moses de—10
Letter of Aristeas—97
letters—127
liberty—83, 86
Light unto the Eyes—97
liturgy—35
Loanz, Jacob ben Jehiel—11
love—75, 192
Luria, Isaac ben Solomon—10
Luther, Martin—20, 153

macrocosm—76
Magnus, Albertus—57
man—53, 60, 66-69, 76, 77, 79, 80, 90-92, 95, 100, 108, 110, 119, 120, 122, 159, 190, 192
Mantua—97, 99
Maimonidean—189
Maimonides—2, 3, 8, 19, 30, 32, 37, 100-102, 121, 122, 126, 187, 192
majority—82
male—75
malkut zadon—85
marranos—152
marriage—75
Martin IV, Pope—9
material—74, 190
mathematics—20
Maximilian II, King—36
mean, golden—130
Meisel, Mordecai—28, 38
Melling, Isaac, Rabbi—17, 38, 39
Meor Enayim—82, 97, 99, 131
Messiah—8, 9, 154-156, 162, 171, 177
Messiah, ben Joseph—10
Messianic, Age—164
Messianic, redemption—10
Messianic, speculations—171
metaphysics—3, 101, 108, 115, 116, 189
Metatron—64

microcosm—76
midrash—57
Mill, John Stuart—83
mind—136
miracles—112, 113, 161
Mirandola, Pico della—11
Mishnah—38, 45, 95, 130, 137, 143
Moravia—35, 43, 47, 135
Moravian Jewry—36
Moore, George Foote—162
morality—109, 118, 182
Mosaic law—158
Moses—107, 116, 121, 122, 124, 131, 157, 158, 192
Moses, religion of—161
Moses ben Nahman—8
Muelhausen, Yom Tob Lippman—36, 37
Muenster, Sebastian—154
mysticism—1, 23, 56, 60, 152, 187, 193
mysticism, Jewish—12
mysticism, Christian—129
mystics—134, 188
mystics, Christian—57

"nadler" calumny—17, 41
Nahmanides—19, 156, 192
nation—86, 172, 191
nationalism—30, 194
nationality—27
natural place—172, 173, 191
nature—66, 103, 105, 112, 117, 129, 134, 167, 173
neo-Platonism—12, 192
neo-Platonists—193
Ner-Mitzvah—48, 49
Netibot Olam—48
New Testament—155, 158
Nezah Yisrael—48
Nicolsberg—35, 36
Nizahon—37
Noahite laws—183

[208]

non-existence—176
non-Jews—88, 182
numbers—7, 130

obscurantism—32
Or Hadash—48
other-worldliness—161

pagan—88
Pahad Yitzhak—46
Palestine—8-10, 33, 139, 172
Paracelsus—11, 57, 129
paradise—115
Pardes Rimonim—11
Paris—134
particulars—194
Paul—162
Paulus Fagius—154
peace—80
Pearl—20
perfection—69, 70, 73, 90, 117, 119
Perles, Meir—20
persecutions—18, 36, 102, 168
Philo—97
philosophers—104, 109
philosophy—2, 3, 108, 121
physical—95
physics—20, 101
piety—2, 109, 190
pilpul—19, 45, 46, 133, 137, 138, 190
Pinhas of Koretz, Rabbi—1
Plato—23, 135
Platonism—134
P'ne Yitzhak—46
Poland—28, 30, 33, 34, 42, 48, 138
polemics—152, 153
Polish Jewry—12, 29
Pollack, Jacob—45
Pomponazzi—31
Posen—18, 30, 43, 48
Prague—21, 33, 36, 37, 39, 41, 43, 45-48, 143, 151, 153
Prausnitz—35

prayer—119
printing—37
prophecy—9, 106, 116, 123, 124, 160
prophets—107, 158
Protestantism—24, 26, 28, 153
providence—106, 115, 159
Provincali, Moses—98
Purim—164
Pythagoras—128

Raba—57
rabbinate—34, 36, 40, 41, 43, 138, 139
rabbis—124, 125, 179, 181-183
Rashi—19, 46, 136, 139, 140
rationalism—3, 99-101, 104, 110, 133, 134, 187, 192
rationalism, Talmudic—135
rationalists—112, 113, 120, 126
religion—161, 189
reality—188
reason—2, 95, 100, 107, 110, 111, 115, 117, 144, 160
Recanti, Menahem di—11
Reformation—29, 153
Remus, Peter—134
Rennaissance—22, 193
retribution—158, 159, 160
Reuchlin, John—11
revelation—102, 115, 116, 165
Rosenberg, Yudel—58
Rossi, Azariah dei—82, 97, 131
Rudolph II, Emperor—47
Russia—138

Saadia—8, 100
Sabbath—119
sacrifices—95, 163
Safed—10, 11, 99
salvation—162
Sammael—64
Samson—19
Satan—64

FROM THE WORLD OF THE CABBALAH

Saxony—28
scholasticism—187, 188, 189
Scholem, Gershom G.—4
science—31, 102, 103, 104, 105, 108, 115, 116, 181, 182, 187, 188, 194
Sefer Emunah—154
Sefer ha-Maalot—11
Sefer Yezirah—7, 9, 127, 130
Sefirot—3, 4, 5, 6, 7, 8, 9, 12, 64, 65, 66, 76, 111, 130
self-government, Jewish—33, 39, 40
Septuagint—97
sex—74, 75, 76
Shekinah—169
Shema—179, 180
Shiur Komah—7
Shir ha-Yihud—44
Shomer Emunim—57
Shulhan Aruk—143
Simeon ben Johai—10
sin—91
Sinai—19, 130
society—84
soul—67, 68, 108, 112, 118
soul of Torah—126, 127
Socratic philosophy—135
Spain—12, 33
spheres—110
state—85
suffering—167
Sylvester, John, Cardinal—151
syllogistic reasoning—188

Talmud—2, 8, 26, 31, 34, 44, 57, 64, 70, 71, 74, 97, 101, 102, 129, 144, 151, 153, 155, 156, 162, 164, 178, 179, 182, 184
Talmud, burning of—153
Talmudic law—180
Talmudists—123, 181

Temple—176
Tetragrammaton—26
theosophy—128
Tiferet Yisrael—48
time—63, 64, 175-177
Titus—98, 131
Torah—2, 3, 4, 18, 40, 68, 95, 101, 106, 116, 117, 120, 121, 125, 126, 128, 154, 161, 166, 177, 190
Torah, oral—123, 124, 125
Tosefot—136
Tosefot Yom Tob—38
trade—136 137
trinity—12
truth—81, 82, 122
tuition fees—144
Turkey—33

universals—188, 194
universe—90, 106, 116
unity—81

vacations—141
Vital, Chaim—10

wine, non-Jewish—32, 42, 43, 174
"work of creation"—6
"work of the chariot"—6
world—61
Worms—18
worship—35

Xenophon—135

Zaddic—193
Zaddic, ibn—192
Zaleshovska, Catherine—30
Zera, Rab—57
Zohar—1, 5, 10, 12, 19